AN
ENCYCLOPEDIA
OF
SEVEN

7

MARTY COOLING

ISBN: 1469974312
ISBN-13: 9781469974316
Library of Congress Control Number: 2012903122
CreateSpace, North Charleston, SC

"*I doubt whether anyone could adequately celebrate the properties of the number seven, for they are beyond all words. Yet the fact that it is more wondrous than all that is said about it is no reason for maintaining silence regarding it. Nay, we must make a brave attempt to bring out all that is within the compass of our understanding, even if it be impossible to bring out all or even the most essential points.*"

Philo of Alexandria, 20 BCE – 50 CE

With special thanks to:

Heidi Cooling, my personal IT department; Preston Cooling, chief proof reader; Charles William Johnson, for help on enneagrams; Stan Pumf, for use of his numerous 77 Facts About the Number 7; Keiko Watanabe, for her help on Japanese traditions, folklore, and adages; Leonard G. Leverson, for generously sharing his lecture on Sabbaticals, Jubilee, and Release; Joseph Meyer, for help on music; the late Bill Culbertson, for his knowledge of telephone companies and Braille; and all the many others who shared their stories and knowledge.

✳

TABLE OF CONTENTS

INTRODUCTION

Seven – what's the first thing that comes to mind? Is it your lucky number? Do you think of the Seven Wonders of the World? How about 7UP? Maybe Snow White and the seven dwarfs. Or Noah's ark. As for me, not being superstitious, a gambler, into mathematics or a deep thinker of any sort, I would have probably started with seven days of the week. But recently as the number kept coming up in conversations, on product labels, and in things I was reading – I realized there was just a lot of seven things. So I started making a list and couldn't stop. This book is the result.

What I found was that I am not the only one thinking seven crops up in a lot of odd places and there are a lot of septomaniacs around. If you are one yourself, this book is dedicated to you. If you just want to have a handy quick reference guide for trivia games and crosswords, feel free to skip directly to the section of lists. For the bar-bet affectiondos, you may find a few tidbits of information that fellow tidbitsters are not likely to know. Or if, like me you have an obsession with listing and obscure fact gathering, this will be a fun addition to your library.

We'll have some fun, learn some new things, and never think about seven the same way again. Old Philo (see quote above) nailed this one.

Chapter 1

SCIENCE AND MATH

SEVEN IS A unique number in the fields of science and mathmatics. In this chapter we will explore a variety of occurances of seven and what makes it different from other numbers. We will also look at bits of trivia of the number seven as found in these areas.

Seven Bits of Memory

Harvard grad George A. Miller, besides being a leader in American psychology, had an elegant way with words. Here's the first paragraph of a famous article he wrote:

My problem is that I have been persecuted by an integer. For seven years this number has followed me around, has intruded in my most private data, and has assaulted me from the pages of our most public journals. This number assumes a variety of disguises, being sometimes a little larger and sometimes a little smaller than usual, but never changing so much as to be unrecognizable. The persistence with which this number plagues me is far more than a random accident. There is, to quote a famous senator, a design behind it, some pattern governing its

appearances. Either there really is something unusual about the
number or else I am suffering from delusions of persecution. [1]

What his theory breaks down to is this: people can't keep more
than about seven bits of random information in their short-term
memory. We can increase the actual amount of information if we
group like things together and just remember the group as a whole.
For instance, you could remember "alphabet" rather than all of the individual letters and "HOMES" instead of each of the Great Lakes and
"siblings" for the names of all your brothers and sisters. For example,
by remembering that your thirteen siblings all live beside the either
Lake Huron, Lake Ontario, Lake Michigan, Lake Erie, and Lake Superior and were named Amos, Bertha, Carrie, Darma, Ephron, Franco,
George, Heidi, ImmaJean, Jill, Kyla, Louise, and Merlon, you only have
to know three bits of information instead of about forty-five.

Now I haven't been able to prove anything, and Ma Bell isn't talking, but it wasn't long after Miller published his theory that telephone
numbers suddenly jumped from being three to five digits to seven. My
very good inside authority says the phone company would have made
the numbers longer, but they didn't think customers would be able to
remember them.

Was Miller the first to publish this theory? Not by several hundred
years. "Nobody can remember more than seven of anything," said
Cardinal Robert Bellarmine, who lived from 1542 to 1621. He used this
as his excuse for omitting the eight beatitudes from his catechism.

pH 7

The *p* in *pH* stands for *potenz*, German for concentration. Not
the thinking kind, but the kind that tells you about purity. Not the
chaste kind of purity, but rather the kind that may tell you how many
parts of something are contained in the whole as compared to the
whole. (Some easy things just can't be explained easily). The *H* is for
hydrogen ion. (At least that was easy.) pH then, is a measure of the
concentration of protons in a solution, so that we know if the stuff is
acid-y or alkaline-y. This is a measure devised by Danish chemist S. P.

L. Sorensen back about the turn of the last century. He made a scale of 0 (which would be very, very one way) through 14 (very, very the other way.) I always forget which is which. So just remember that usually seven is good and neutral. Seven isn't acidic or basic either. This is what your blood needs to be to sustain life—if the pH drops below 7.0 or rises above 7.8, well, it just isn't pretty.

But isn't it curious that Sorensen made the scale 0 through 14? Why did he do that? Actually, he did have a method to his madness. Sorensen began with the knowledge that pure water has hydrogen ion concentration of 1×10^{-7} moles, which is a balance of positively charged ions and negatively charged ones. (In chemistry, a mole is a gram molecule.) Acidic water had a hydrogen ion concentration of 1×10^0 and alkaline water was 1×10^{14}. So his scale of 0–14, with 7 being the median, was defined by nature.

And for the record, pH in the acid range is 0–7 and the alkaline range is 7–14. I looked it up again so you won't have to—just in case you also never can remember which way is which.

Circaseptennial Rhythms

The Greek ancients—they really were quite advanced in their science—concluded that many things in our world cycled in seven-year time spans. They thought this especially true in human growth. Alas, though, they hedged by adding *circa*, which means "about," giving them a year or so on either side for error.

A couple of men from Europe rather recently decided to test this theory by measuring the growth patterns of Englishmen's ears. (Did you *know* that your ears don't ever stop growing?) Sure enough, the researchers discovered ear-growth in Englishmen peaks every seven years. They followed up with studies of other interesting and obscure circaseptennial rhythms. They wrote: "Around 1980 or so, [Verhulst] noted that physicists involved in the development of quantum mechanics were born in four 7-year waves [also] Nobel physicists. These top physicians also tend to be born in the 7n+4 years. . . . Prominent statisticians show a very pronounced tendency to be born in years belonging to the 7n+2 phase (years that produce remainder 2 when divided by 7)." [2]

And in the growth of our sculls, "Where the flat bones in the skull meet, there are sutures where growth can still occur. . . . It became clear to me that accelerations of the process of suture closing occurred [each seven years.]" [3] Let's believe in our hearts that this is the scientific breakthrough that will lead to increasing longevity, permanent world health improvements, and a peaceful universe.

Even these men are not the only ones to notice sevens in cycles of our flora and fauna. Theologian Kenneth Westby writes, "By surprise, science has discovered amazing seven-day cycles in the very building blocks of plant and animal life. These newly found sevens, or 'septans,' also lie buried in us humans—deep in our metabolic, hormonal, and neuronal networks."[4]

Donald R. Barber's 1997 article "The Origin of the Seven Year Biological Cycle and the Expanding Universe" says: "The existence of a physically real seven-year biological cycle in avian song and human basal heart-rate records was revealed by studies made by the author in the years 1959-68. This . . . shows the interval in days between the dates of starting and finishing seasonal song . . . of the common Chaffinch for each of the years 1946-68. The seven year cycle is clearly seen." [5]

The Seven Processes of the Hydrologic Cycle

Water is amazing stuff. It moves from the ground to the air and back and from a liquid to a solid to a gas and back again. The hydrologic cycle is this exchange of form and involves seven processes. They are condensation, evaporation, infiltration, percolation, precipitation, runoff, and transpiration. Condensation occurs when water in its gaseous form cools off and becomes either a solid (hail, sleet, snow) or a liquid (rain, dew.) When condensation leads to one of the things that falls out of the air, we call it precipitation. Whenever the falling stuff manages to get all the way to the ground and seeps in, it is called infiltration. The water then percolates down through the sand, soil, and rocks until the space is filled up and gravity pulls it into an aquifer, an underground stream, a well, or a lower spot of ground where it would fill a lake, pond, or river. If the water for whatever reason doesn't soak into the ground, it can run right over the surface until it finds its lowest point, which is what we call run-off.

At a lot of these points, the water will heat up again and be returned to the atmosphere by evaporation. Water can also be returned to a gas by transpiration. That is when plants excrete the water from leaves and back it goes into its gas form. When this happens on people, we call it perspiration. Fun stuff.

Seven Colors of the Rainbow

If you have ever heard either the name "Roy G. Biv" or the phrase "Richard Of York Gave Battle In Vain," you may recall that they are mnemonics to help us remember the colors of the rainbow in order: red, orange, yellow, green, blue, indigo and violet. Isaac Newton is credited for naming the colors of the rainbow in the spectrum in 1671. He defined the spectrum as "all those colors that consist of visible light of a single wavelength only, the pure spectral or monochromatic colors." He was a smart guy.

The Periodic Chart

You will find that most periodic tables have seven rows, or periods. The elements in a period have valence electrons in the same "shell." The number of valence electrons increase from left to right on the individual rows and they share common chemical properties. The seven rows include metals, semi-conductors, non-metals, and inert gasses. (We'll omit the lanthanides and actinides for this discussion, as they do not occur naturally.)

Let's talk a bit about group VII. This group is made up of the halogens—fluorine, chlorine, bromine, iodine, and astatine. They all have seven electrons in the outer shell. "They are choking poisonous gases." That's all I have to say about that.

When you are talking about the elements, a *heptad* is defined as an "atom which has a valence of seven, and which can be theoretically combined with, substituted for, or replaced by, seven monad atoms or radicals." If a heptad has seven units of attractive force, or affinity, it is heptavalent.

Seven Metals of Antiquity

From the first recorded history until not so long ago, only seven metals were known to exist. (Today we know of eighty-six, but until the nineteenth century, the count was twenty-four, and half of those were identified just the century before.)

The very first metal to be found in nature was gold, which was known about 6000 BC by the Mesopotamians, Greeks, Romans, and Egyptians, and probably others. And what do you suppose they did with gold? The same thing we do today—make jewelry. Gold is great for this, as it is found naturally, often in pure form, is so malleable that it can be pounded into very, very, very thin sheets or pulled into long thin wires, and it stays gorgeous and gold without tarnishing.

Copper is almost as old, having been known and used for about the last seven thousand years. It too was used for jewelry, but when it was discovered that heating made copper very strong, it was then used for tools and weapons.

Silver is also found in nature just the way it is, but it's hard to find. It's not quite as soft as gold and tends to tarnish, but because of its rarity and malleability, it was also used in jewelry.

Lead was a tricky metal and not found just laying around. It was probably first used when galena, which looks like metal, was discovered to separate from its ore by very little heat. Then, too, it was found to be easily molded into whatever shape was needed.

Tin came about a thousand years later. It was used in combination with other metals to make them strong.

Iron was found in meteors. They must have had half the world out looking for meteors—after all, how many have you ever seen? But find it they did, and iron's use as weapons and tools changed the way those ancients lived.

Mercury, or quicksilver, showed up about 1500 BC, and is the only metal that is a liquid at room temperature. These people knew how to make things very, very hot, but not how to get them very cold. So for all they knew, mercury was a liquid and that was that. There wasn't much they could do with the stuff, so they mostly just looked at it.

Sometime later it was used to dissolve silver and gold, but why that was a good thing, I cannot say.

Seven Crystal Systems

"The crystal system is the point group of the lattice (the set of rotation and reflection symmetries which leave a lattice point fixed,) not including the positions of the atoms in the units cell."[6] Boom. Don't you be asking me that again. (Actually, I took that explanation from Wikipedia, which has a way of explaining things so they are easily understood.) There are seven different crystal systems – isometric, tetragonal, rhombohedral, hexagonal, orthorhombic, monoclinic, and triclinic. Hopefully, by the time someone asks me this question I'll have the seven memorized or will have mastered my finest "good grief – if you don't know *this*, what *do* you know?" look and hope they go away.

Seven Miles per Second

That's how fast you have to go to leave the earth's atmosphere.

The Seven Keplerian Elements

Have you wanted to plot the orbit of a satellite? You'll need a set of seven numbers to do this, and Johann Kepler, who lived from 1571 to 1630, defined them for us. Professor Miguel Calvo Ramon of the Universidad Politecnica de Madrid does a nice job of explaining this so that we can understand it:

* Epoch—The set of orbital elements is a snapshot, at a particular time, of the orbit of a satellite. Epoch is simply a number which specifies the time at which the snapshot was taken.

* Orbital inclination—The orbit ellipse lies in a plane known as the orbital plane. The orbital plane always goes through the center of the earth, but may be tilted any angle relative to the equator. Inclination is the angle between the orbital plane and the equatorial plane.

✳ Right ascension of ascending node—This is the second number that will give us the plane of the orbit. A node is the point at which the orbit of the satellite intersects the plane of the orbit of its planet. Since this will occur twice, use only the one that is ascending (where the crossover goes north.) Now that we have this point, we want the angle from here to the center of the planet. And please use the astronomical coordinate system instead of latitude and longitude.

✳ Argument of perigee—(Don't you just love these terms? If it sounds like Greek, it is.) An argument, Ramon tells us, is "a fancy word for angle." Perigee is the point nearest to the planet in the orbit of the satellite. So what we want to do now is find the angle where the Angle of Nodes intersects with the line of apsis. The line of apsis is "just a line drawn through the ellipse the 'long way.'"

✳ Eccentricity—Again from Ramon: "This one is simple. In the Keplerian orbit model, the satellite orbit is an ellipse. Eccentricity tells us the 'shape' of the ellipse." Actually, it is the deviation from a true circle, i.e., how flattened out the orbit is.

✳ Mean motion—This number tells us how far away the satellite is. Basically, the closer a satellite is to the planet, the faster it spins. The further away, the slower it spins. So just find the average of the fastest and the slowest to derive the mean motion.

✳ Mean anomaly—As with mean motion, mean anomaly is another average. Anomaly, super-simplified in this context, is just angle. This number will tell us *where* on the orbit our satellite is at the given moment we defined in epoch. [7]

Tracking satellites is not as obscure a pastime as you may think. Just ask your neighbor who is a ham radio enthusiast. On the other hand, elements for most of the commonly used satellites are posted numerous places. Sometimes it's just interesting to find out *how* all of this is done.

A NUMBER OF THINGS

MAN HAS FOUND it necessary to count for a very long time. And of course, people have found different ways to say or write a numeral that means the quantity of seven. It is not surprising that through the ages mankind has used all sorts of numbering systems. Probably the first was a unary method, a system that uses a single symbol to represent *all* the numbers, and only by repetition would the quantity be apparent. Actually, for some things, it still serves a good purpose and is used by all of us as when we hold up fingers or carve the daily hash marks on our cell walls. Say you are counting certain objects and continuously find more. You *could* add the newest count to the previous one, and mark out the old number, but whew, it's just too darn easy to lose track. So how about just keeping a running count that you can add on to and add up the total easily when you are all done? We do this all the time with tallies—those hash marks we all make. In the United States, it is customary for us to group these mark in bunches of five—four hashes and a slash. This arrangement makes it easier to count up the total when we are through, since most of us can count by fives without too much difficulty. Seven expressed in tally is ℍℍ II.

As we became more sophisticated, we started giving the numbers names, and often used the letters of the alphabet. The Romans, Indians (the ones with dots, not feathers) and Hebrews all had numbering systems that used letter-names for numbers. But with most of these systems, you still had to total up the quantities because they didn't use place values.

Along the way, men figured out some fast and easy ways to do calculations, though, and you didn't even have to know the names for the numbers. One incredible method used by the Chinese long before the abacus was called counting rods—sort of a sophisticated tally system. The rods were small sticks. When using counting rods, the digits one through nine are each expressed two different ways. Depending on the decimal position, you can distinguish the numbers from each other—after all, tally marks all look pretty much the same. The number 7 in this system would be either π, or $\doteq$. So, 7,777 would have been written $\frac{\perp}{\pi}\frac{\perp}{\pi}$. It would seem that two ways to write numbers would only be necessary for 1 through 5, since 6 through 9 are bundled, but I'm leaving that alone.

The suan phan abacus that we think of the Chinese using was not the first. The Romans also used an abacus and were able to do long, complex calculations quickly. The one used by Romans had fourteen bars or wires—seven short ones and seven long ones. The short bars had a single bead and the long ones had four beads.

Crossing Our Sevens

Here it is, friends and neighbors, the burning question of the ages: How come the folks in Europe put a cross on their number 7 and Americans don't? And the answer is—well, we don't really know. Many times we can't explain what *Americans* do, so how are we ever supposed to understand what the Europeans are up to? Here's the most prevalent hypothesis, as explained by Doctor Tom of "Ask Dr. Math" (The Math Forum is a research and educational enterprise of Drexel University). "The line is to distinguish it from the numeral '1'. Most Europeans draw a '1' not with just a vertical line, but with a tiny stroke from the top and down to the left. If you're writing quickly, it's easy to mix it up with a '7'."

That explains why Europeans use the cross, but doesn't mention why Americans *don't*. So let's back up to the history of our numbering system. The system we use is Arabic, which dates back, oh, several thousand years. The BBC website the Guide to Life, The Universe and Everything says this about the numerals: "The shapes of our numerals originally had a striking significance. Each single digit numeral contained the number of angles it named." So, when first devised, the written numeral 7 had seven angles.

Over the years, we have dropped the hangy-down thing on the top and the foot-thing on the bottom, reducing the number of angles to five. And we Americans, in our efforts at simplicity, have also dropped the cross in the middle, taking away another four. I suppose, since we also stopped putting the flag on number 1, we thought 7 didn't look like 1 anymore, so the cross in the middle wasn't needed to make the distinction. I'm only guessing here, because no one else can really say.

But look at what we are starting to do again: we're putting the cross back. Don't you see this more all the time? Maybe we think it makes us appear more continental (I'm just guessing at this too). Or maybe we just like to cross things now, like to distinguish between *o* and *O* and *Z* and 2. So what's it going to hurt?

Roman Numerals

Long before we started using the Arabic numbers, we had the Roman numerals. It wasn't too bad as far as things go, but the system lacked the all-important zero (a few more of which we would all like to see on our paychecks, right? Which reminds me of the geeky slang for making serious money: "a telephone number salary." Seven digits, get it? It also makes me think about "cimicic" and "cimicid," which both have seven letters and are the longest words in English that can be written using only the Roman numerals. I digress—but isn't it these little things that are so much fun?).

The Romans used letters to represent numbers and, low and behold, there were only seven: I, V, X, L, C, D, and M, which represented 1, 5, 10, 50, 100, 500 and 1,000 respectively. Since there are obviously many more numbers than this, they just repeated these as many times as they needed, making you add them all up to find out what number was intended. (It was only much later that this process was shortened by the "subtractive method," which let you subtract the smaller numbers whenever they appeared *before* a larger one. Boom. This surely made things simpler. Just look at the Roman numerals on the credits of some old movie and think how hard it would be to figure out what year it was filmed without this easy method.) *Seven* written in Roman numerals is VII: 5 plus 1 plus 1. I would think you could also write it IIIX because using the subtractive method, that would be 10 minus 3. Except there was a little rule that says you can only subtract the next-highest letter/number. So you can't subtract I's from X's or C's, but only from V's. And you can only subtract V's from X's and X's from C's and so on. And you can only subtract one numeral at a time. Those Romans must have wanted to count really badly to go to all that work, but a lot of documentation shows they weren't really all that picky about any of their own rules. You want to write 7 as IIIIIII? You wouldn't be the first Roman to do that, you wouldn't be very wrong, and somehow they got it all figured out.

The Romans were not the only, or even the first folks to use their alphabet letters to write their numbers—the Armenians and Greeks did, too.

All the Bases

Today when we count and calculate (mathy things that ruined my GPA and still makes my eyes glaze over) we usually use base 10. Isn't that a good choice? Look what happens to our beloved 7 when we start messing around with other bases: if we were using base 2, (which we actually do all the time in the computer-language of binary code, but it's all hidden, so we don't have to think about it) 7 is 111; in base 3 it is 21; in base 4, 13; base 5 would make it 12; base 6 makes it 11, and in septenary base 7, it is 10.

I have heard that at one time, people actually did use base 7 as the standard counting system. They did not survive.

The First Double-Syllable Number

Ever notice that seven is the first and only cardinal number in English that has more than one syllable? Why do you think that is? One of my Internet buddies says that a few years ago, there was a movement to change the pronunciation to one syllable. They were suggesting *sevn*. (Which is still *almost* two syllables.) I've heard some tall tales and this sounds like one of the preposterous things you find on the Internet. You can write any darn thing you want and someone will believe it. And who knows? There's just no telling what is important to some people, so maybe there is some truth to it. Or maybe this guy's just yanking my chain.

Numerology

Numerology can be loosely defined as the study of the meanings of numbers, a practice that has been used in many different cultures for a long, long time.

If you are numerologically a 7, Joseph Ghabi of the Free Spirit Centre (he's asked me to pass along his website for those interested in more details: http://freespiritcentre.info) says this about you:

> *Seven is a very good number. A lucky number but the one[s] who have that number being alone is also part of who they are. That does not mean they have to live alone. Seven is an inward number where the individuals who have need to learn about trust (in themselves) and believe (in the universe) issues. ... They are very gifted people and they know, but they are scared of it.*

COMPUTER/GADGETY THINGS

Seven-Segment Display

Does this look familiar?

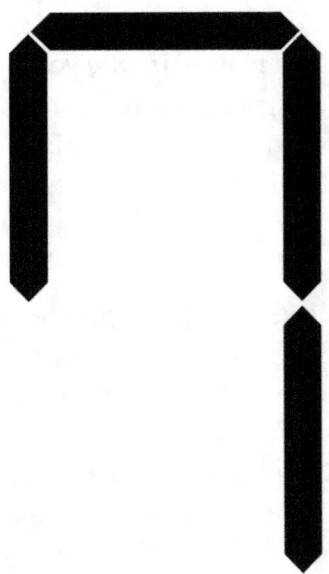

TAKE A CLOSE look at an old digital clock. Or the readout screen of your cheap calculator. Or anything else that has a light-emitting diode (LED) readout with those lines that form the numbers. (C'mon—this *is* the twenty-first century, and this technology is already outdated.) Every number and letter is made up of combinations of seven straight lines by turning certain of the little lights either on or off. It works fairly well, even though some of the letters are a little contrived, like when they are using capital letters and then come to G (which is the seventh letter, by the way), which doesn't fit, so they switch to lower case. But still in all, it's a very efficient way to format the numbers. And being square, the numbers are almost identical to the ones first used by the Arabs.

Signaling System Seven—a.k.a. SS7, a.k.a. C7

Any telephone system in today's world needs a signaling mechanism "to set up and tear down the calls." Examples of signals are the telephone's ringing, the dial tone, your phone connecting to the local connecting office, caller ID, and routing of toll-free numbers. There are many more but they all serve basically three functions – supervising, alerting, and addressing calls. The SS7 uses a dedicated sixty-four kilobit data circuit to carry digital packet data and has been the standard since 1987. The ability to bundle information digitally and squirt it through the telephone lines during the minute pauses in our voice conversations is the breakthrough that not only speeds up the system but allows all the added features like credit-card calling, "roaming," call forwarding, call waiting, and conference calling.

ASCII Seven-Bit Code

Almost all of the computers we use have used the American Standard Code for Information Interchange (ASCII) since 1963 as a code to decipher the information from the on/off, or +/-, or 1/0 settings of binary language that the computer translates into some readable format that *we* can read. ASCII is explained by Wikipedia, as "a seven-bit code, meaning that it uses the bit patterns representable with seven binary digits ... to represent character information." (Isn't that what I just said?) It was "developed from telegraphic codes and its first commercial use was as a 7-bit teleprinter code promoted by Bell data services."

The binary code uses a series of eight on/off switches we call bits. The on/off sequence of each bite, the group of eight, represents a letter, a number, or a code—for instance olll llll (all seven digits "on") means "delete." The number 7, then, is coded 0000 0111.

Seven-Layer Model

The seven-layer model is a set of protocols used in network architecture, so we can do things like play on the Internet. Also known as the Open Systems Interconnection (OSI) reference model, it was designed so that each layer uses the one below it and serves the one above. "Protocols enable an entity in one host to interact with a corresponding entity at the same layer in a remote host." [8] Evidently, this is a good thing. From the lowest to the top, here are the seven layers:

* Physical

* Data link

* Network

* Transport

* Session

* Presentation

* Application

Actually, this sequence is applicable only if you are *receiving* data. If you are *transmitting*, please reverse the order or who knows what is going to happen to all that nice data?

The Ampersand (&)

Anyone who types, or keyboards as we computer-users say it nowadays, makes the ampersand by capitalizing the 7 key. Computer geeks, renowned for their sense of humor (not) and reluctance to abbreviate everything, call this *and* sign a "shift-7."

Sub-seven Virus—a.k.a. SubSeven 2.0 Server, Pinkworm, Backdoor Trojan

A few years ago, waaaaay back in 1999, a computer virus in the form of a Trojan horse, was spammed around the world to users of Microsoft Windows. A Trojan horse is a program that is purported (by the spammer/sender) to have some useful feature (such as nude photographs of Jennifer Lopez or a video of Timothy McVeigh's execution) but actually contains a payload of mischief that would grant hackers use of your computer. Technically, since the sub-seven virus did not replicate, it wasn't a virus. It didn't cause too much damage and was rather easy, by comparison, to remove. But it was one of the first and best, and we will all remember it fondly.

GEOMETRY

Heptagon

Before we begin, I have promised all those cranky math teachers to help get one thing perfectly clear: *we do not use Latin roots when describing shapes.* So all you people who keep saying "multigon" instead of "polygon" are probably the same rebels saying "septagon" instead of "heptagon." While you may be just as correct as can be etymologically, you still need to stop that. It makes mathematicians angry. They are a tough bunch of folks we don't want to get riled up. So let's indulge them and no one will get hurt.

Now that we have taken care of that little bit of business, we shall state that a heptagon is a seven-sided two-dimensional figure. A heptagon also has seven angles, of course.

Heptagonal Triangles

A heptagonal number is a figurate number that represents a heptagon. Seven is the second heptagonal number, and we know this, of course, because the formula to find them is $n(5n - 3)/2$, with $n > 0$. "A figurate number is one that can be represented as a regular and discrete geometric pattern (e.g. dots)." [9] Seven is also the second *centered* hexagonal number. That's one that is a figurate number that represents a hexagon with a dot in the center and all the other dots surrounding the center dot equidistantly. I feel in my heart that this will be the most important information in this book to someone. So, for the rest of you, thanks for listening.

If you are looking for something to fill up your afternoon, try creating an equilateral heptagon within a circle using a compass and straight edge. Don't spend too much time on this. It cannot be done. To put it more eloquently, seven is the first number that does not enter in the Euclidian circle—the heptagon cannot be scribed in a circle of 360 degrees as can a triangle or a pentagon. This is perhaps one of the most unique things about the number seven. Maybe it would work if we used a circle with less than 360 degrees. . .

Seven Bundled Rods

While you are at it, or on some other afternoon when you don't have anything to do, try putting a rubber band around seven pencils. Notice anything unusual? Probably not, so take one out. See any difference? Now try eight pencils. Or nine or four. Funny stuff, huh?

Since you already have your seven pencils out, here's a puzzle that has occupied people for quite some time. The object is to arrange all seven pencils so that each one touches each other one. Go ahead and try it. I'll wait.

Well, if you are going to be slow about this, perhaps the rest of us had better get moving along. But don't feel bad if you can't figure it out right away—I've seen math professors from major universities take a while too.

Triangles

There are seven names for triangles. The two ways you can describe a triangle are by its sides or by its angles. If you are describing by the sides, there are three—*equilateral*, which means all three sides are the same length, or *isosceles*, which means two of the sides are the same length, or *scalene*, which means all three sides are different lengths. If you name triangles by their angles, there are four: *equiangular*, when the angles are all the same, a *right-angle* triangle, for when one of the angles is 90 degrees, *obtuse* describes a triangle that has one angle more than 90 degrees, and an *acute* triangle is one that has all three angles less than 90 degrees.

BY THE NUMBERS

THE WORD *SEVEN* is most often used as a cardinal number. Let's just take a moment to think about this and appreciate the full import. "Most often" has been calculated as 99.82 percent of the time, according to Webster's Online Dictionary. Why they keep track of such things is one of the mysteries of the Internet. Someone (or some*thing*) is out there actually calculating the frequency of internet keyword searches. The most frequently used seven-search is for "sub seven"—which you folks ask for 2,592 times. Per day. Actually, most of those searches were probably me.

Seven is used about 17,332 times out of a sample of 100 million words spoken or written in English. Its rank is based on over 700,000 words used in the English language.

Multiplication and Division

1 / 7 = .142857142857142857

If you multiply this quotient by 2 you get .285714; if multiplied by 3 the result is .428571; if by 4, .571428; by 5, .714285; by 6, .857142. This is one of the very most unique things about this number. Funny stuff, isn't it?

By extension, 999,999 divided by 7 equals 142,857.

Now divide 360 by 7. You get 51.428571. At first blush, if you people are paying any attention to this at all, you will notice that the sequence—428571—seems to appear quite a bit. I asked you to use 360 this time, because that is the number of degrees in a circle. And as we have talked about already, you cannot divide a circle into seven neat even little pieces. That didn't sound so surprising to me until I threw some numbers in a spreadsheet and saw all the other numbers from 1 to 10 dividing up so nicely – 360,180,120, 90, 72, 60, 45, 40—and then there's the 7 divisor with the dividend of 51.428571.

The number 22 has been closely associated with circles. If this sounds goofy, the history of the correlation comes from a couple of places: "The number 22 is considered symbolic of a complete circle ... because this is reflected by the twenty-two letters in the Hebrew alphabet, the twenty-two keys in the Major Arcana of the Tarot...and indicate[s] the full circle of experience." [10] "So what?" you cry. Divide 22 by 7. The result is 3.1428571. (Notice our now-favorite number sequence of 428571) But what else do you see? Yes, you math geeks! Dividing 22 by 7 gives you pi. Pi is like the second most interesting number in the universe!

Because the repeating block has six numbers, which is one less than seven, a prime, that makes seven a golden prime.

7 to the 7th power = 523,543

The Magic Number Seven

Want to play? Log on to mdani.demon.co.uk/stunt/nov96s1.htm. Go ahead—take your time. This book is already written so I can wait.

Done? That was fun and clever, wasn't it? Dr. Michael Daniels is a fun and clever guy. He is with the school of psychology at Liverpool John Moores University. Now, since he says his "psychic powers" were used to give you the answer, and he put *psychic powers* in quotes, we know that he knows he doesn't really have them. So how *did* he do it? He's such a nice guy that he gave me permission to tell you: "The trick works because any whole number divided by seven (other than a multiple of seven) will give a remainder made of the digit sequence 142857 (Don't ask why!) This sequence then recurs, e.g. 142857142857142857 etc. Depending on the number to be divided, the sequence will start with a different digit in the same sequence, i.e., 428571, 285714, 857142, 571428, [or] 714285. So when you add the first six digits after the decimal point, the total will always be 27."

Now, if you got lost in all that, you didn't look up the site on the Internet, did you? I know you people. You think I'm going to explain everything and you won't have to do your homework.

When telling me all about this website, he mentioned something else that's funny-weird. He says the missing digits, 3-6-9, are interesting too. He instructs: "Draw a circle and write the numbers 1 to 9 around this, evenly spaced. Then join the points on the circumference with straight lines in the sequence 1-4-2-8-5-7-1. This will then form the shape of the enneagram. The missing 3-6-9 will form a separate triangle."

"All very odd," says Dr. Daniels, and he knows odd.

Ready for more fun? Get out your calculator. One with a seven-segment display readout will be grand, thank you. Enter in any number less than 700. Divide that number by 7. Add the digits to the right of the decimal place. (If there aren't any, try some other number.) If the answer is 27, I win. That's it. Magic.

Link and Chasm

Here's something else unique: multiply 1 x 2 x 3 x 4 x 5 x 6 x 7. You'll get 5,040. Now multiply 7 x 8 x 9 x 10. Still 5,040. According to Michael Schneider, who wrote *A Beginner's Guide to Constructing the Universe, A Voyage from 1 to 10*, this makes the number 7 a "link."

What would happen if you leave 7 out of the computations? 1 x 2 x 3 x 4 x 5 x 6 = 720; 8 x 9 x 10 = 720. This makes 7 a "chasm."

Seven is the only number from 1 to 10 that is either a link or a chasm. And it's both.

Is 689 Evenly Divisible by 7?

Okay, I know this question will probably never, ever come up in your whole long life. But here is an easy way to figure out if *any* number is evenly divisible by 7: take away the last digit, in this case 9, double that number to get 18. Now subtract 18 from the rest of the number. If it is divisible by 7, the entire number will be. If you don't know if it is or not, do it again until you get to a number you know is, or until you get all the way down to 7.

On second thought, perhaps this is not the easiest method, so here's another: take your three-digit number 689; multiply the 6 by 3 to get 18; now add 18 to the second two digits: 18 + 8 + 9 = 35. If the number you get is divisible by 7, the entire three-digit number will be. Yes, this way is definitely easier.

If you have a four-digit number, just take the first digit and multiply by 4, then add all the other digits; if a five-digit number, multiply the first by 5 and do the addition. Pretty cool?

Here's another weird thing. If you repeat a digit six times—like 555,555—that number will always be evenly divisible by 7. I am going to go get a drink (a 7 & 7) while the rest of you think about this phenomenon and try it out with your wee pocket calculator (hopefully the one that has a seven-segment display.)

The same thing happens if you repeat a two-digit number six times—like 434,343,434,343.

This *also* works for repeating three-digit numbers, as with 289,289,289,289,289,289. Some other spooky things happen, pattern-wise, if you extend the one-digit numbers like this:

$111,111 \div 7 = 15,873$

$101,010,101,010 \div 7 = 14,430,014,430$

$100,100,100,100,100,100 \div 7 = 14,300,014,300,014,300$

$100,010,001,000,100,010,001,000 \div 7 = 14,287,143,000,014,287,143,000$

WHAT IS A 7?

Lucky Numbers

A lucky prime is a group of natural numbers discovered by Stanislaw Ulam in 1955. Well, of course he didn't discover the numbers, but he played around with them until some fun stuff happened, and then he labeled those numbers "lucky." He was a modest man, as most folks would have called them Ulam numbers or at least not put up too much of a fuss when his buddies called these numbers Ulams. This is what he did:

Take out a clean piece of paper and write a couple lines of sequential numbers starting with 1. Now cross out all the even numbers, starting with 2. The second number left is 3, so now cross out every third number (but leave 3 alone.) The third number still remaining is now 7, so leave 7, but cross out every remaining seventh number. The ones still there are lucky numbers.

If you are really ambitious, you can now cross out any number that isn't a prime. What you have left now are the lucky primes, and our beloved 7 has made this final cut.

Happy Prime

I'm glad to announce that 7 is the very first happy prime number to be found. And, being a happy prime, it is, of course, also a regular happy number too.

Woodall Number

A Woodall number is a natural number expressed as Wn. The formula for finding Woodall primes is $n \times 2^n - 1$. Since 7 is also a prime number, besides being a Woodall, it is then, by definition, also a Woodall prime. Then, when $n \times bn - 1$, when $n + 2 > b$, it makes the number also a *generalized* Woodall number.

Newman-Shanks-Williams Prime

Seven not only is a Newman-Shanks-Williams prime number, it is the very first one. This is a relatively newfound kind of prime number that was defined by three guys in 1981. They were reportedly studying finite groups with square order at the time. They say that a number is a Newman-Shanks-Williams prime only if it is already a Newman-Shanks-Williams number to begin with. But we've already caught on to that, haven't we?

Mersenne Numbers and Primes

A number is a Mersenne if it has the form "2 to the power of p − 1, if p is prime." We used to believe that all Mersenne numbers are prime, but evidently that isn't so, so we also have:

"A Mersenne prime is a *prime* number that is one less than a power of two. . . . For example, $7 = 8 - 1 = 2^3 - 1$." [11] This is *almost* just like being a perfect number, which is a number that is equal to the sum of its proper divisors. Seven isn't one of the perfect numbers, though, but is almost—because you see, of course, that 6 is.

Carmichael Numbers

This is something 7 is *not*. A Carmichael number is a composite integer "n" if b to the nth power = b (mod n) for every integer b. But, for folks who like to keep track of such things, there are seven such numbers below 10,000: 561; 1,105; 1,729; 2,465; 2,821; 6,601; and 8,911.

There are also only seven *factorial* numbers under 10,000: 1, 2, 6, 24, 120, 720, and 5,040. Factorial is defined "the n-th factorial number is the product of the n first natural numbers. The factorial deserved an exclamation mark for its notation: k! = 1*2*3*...*k." If you have any idea of what that means, then what on earth are you doing reading a lowly book like this?

Deficient

"The number n is deficient if the sum of all its positive divisors except itself is less than n." [12] Seven is one of those numbers.

Lazy Caterer Number

A lazy caterer number is the maximum number of pieces a round pizza can be cut into with n straight-line cuts. Of course, it doesn't have to be a pizza. They just say pizza to distinguish from a cake, which could be cylindrical, which is like a flat pizza on steroids. But since 7 is not a cake number, I'm not going to discuss it.

Narcissistic

Here's the definition of this kind of number: "A k-digit number n is called narcissistic if it is equal to the sum of k-th powers of its digits. They are also called plus perfect numbers." [13] And since every single digit from 1 to 10 is narcissistic, this in no way makes 7 unique—on the other hand, it is a contributing factor, so keep reading.

Odd

An odd number is any one that can't be divided by two evenly. Just thought we needed a little break from all the really complicated stuff.

Odious

If you take an odd number and find it has an odd number of ones in its binary expansion, it is an odious number, as is seven. (If the number of ones is even, the number is then *evil*. Thought you'd all be glad to know that seven is *not* evil.)

Palindromes

As with words and phrases, a number can be a palindrome if it reads the same forward and backward—like 707. For reasons I really can't explain, one-digit numbers are considered palindromic. Personally, I think that's cheating, but there it is. So 7 is a palindrome number. So is 77, and 717, and 77266277, and 7777777, and so forth.

And since I went to all the trouble to find palindromes with "seven" and had no really logical place to put this information, here it is:

* seven eves

* Not seven on a mere man – one vest on

* We seven, Eve, sew

There are also several seven-letter-long one word palindromes: Deified, repaper, reviver, rotator, and racecar.

Palindromic Primes

As you can probably guess, a palindromic prime is any prime number that is a palindrome. So seven fits this description, too. And in base two.

Square-Free Numbers

Seven is square-free because it is not divisible by any square number. Ta da!

Twin Primes

Seven is a twin prime, as are all other prime numbers that have another prime number only two digits away. Five is seven's twin. This is expressed as p, p+2. I'll bet some of you are already thinking about **Prime Triplets**: p, p+2, p+4. There evidently is only one such sequence: 3, 5, 7. Prime triplets, though, is still worth its own definition, so to find more, we can use p, p+4, p+6 (7, 11, 13) or p, p+ 2, p+6 (5, 7, 11.) When calculating any one of these formulas, seven is still caught in the act. **Prime Quadruplets**, then, is a group of four numbers separated thusly: p, p+2, p+6, p+8. Officially, the very first such sequence is 5, 7, 11, and 13. For reasons I won't even pretend to understand, 2, 3, 5, and 7 don't count. Finding patterns such as these of course goes on and on, and it gets really snarky. Probably the only one relevant to this book is the **Prime Septuplets**, which is p, p+2, p+6, p+8, p+12, p+18, and p+20. Sometime in 2004 a guy named Norman Luhn found the largest set of such numbers. It is 1839198074074 * 500# + 165701 + 0, 2, 6, 8, 12, 18, and 20.

What else is a seven? It is a **centered hexagonal number**, a **Columbian**, a **heptagonal**, and a **Wagstaff prime**. There are lots of kinds of numbers. I found 60, actually. And those are only the kinds of numbers that included any integer from 1 to 9. But the vacuuming was done and I had a drink in hand, so I threw them all into a spreadsheet and found that 7 fit into 27 of the categories. Number 1 was #1 with 29 hits; let's give it its due. But our number 7 came in a close second. And I was being very fair by putting in categories of numbers like "evens" and "Ulums" and "Eulers" and "evils" and "repunits." Since not much is really, truly fair and this *is* a book about 7, I then sifted out all the kinds of numbers that 7 is *not*. Now I had a list of 28 kinds of numbers that 7 is, and the closest runner-up is 3, which falls into a mere 18 of the 28. Tsk, tsk.

	1	2	3	4	5	6	7	8	9
centered hexagonal number	x			x					
Columbian number	x		x		x		**x**		x
Deficient	x	x	x	x	x		**x**	x	x
happy number	x						**x**		
happy prime							**x**		
heptagonal number	x						**x**		
lazy caterer	x		x			x			
Lucas number	x		x	x			**x**		
lucky number	x		x				**x**		x
lucky prime		x				x			
Mersenne number		x				x			
Mersenne prime			x				**x**		
narcissistic number	x	x	x	x	x	x	**x**	x	x
Newman-Shanks-Williams prime							**x**		
Odd	x		x		x		**x**		x
odious number	x	x		x			**x**	x	
palindrome number	x	x	x	x	x	x	**x**	x	x
palindromic prime	x	x		x		x			
prime		x	x		x		**x**		
prime quadruplet						x	**x**		
prime triplet			x		x		**x**		
square-free number	x	x		x	x	x			
supersingular prime		x	x		x		**x**		
twin			x		x		**x**		
twin prime		x		x		x			
Wagstaff prime		x		x		x			
Woodall number	x						**x**		
Woodall prime						x			
TOTALS	12	9	18	6	14	3	**28**	4	6

Truly Big Numbers

According to the submitters to Wikipedia, we have named some very, greatly, hugely, unbelievably big, big, numbers. Just in case the national debt rises and we need to talk about it. Here are some of my favorites, although I must tell you that I am relying on all the experts to correct the Wikipedia entries if they are incorrect:

Septillion: symbol = Y; 100 to the 21st power

Sextillion: This has the prefix *zetta*, which is derived from the French *sept*, and is used since it is equal to 1,000 to the 7th power (1,000,000, 000,000,000,000,000,000)

Zepto, symbol *z*, the prefix for a sextillionth, denotes a factor of 10 to the -21st – or $1/1,000^7$ – or 0.000,000,000,000,000,000,001

Yocto, or the prefix for septillionth, is 0.000,000,000,000,000,000,00 0,000,000,001, or $1/1,000^8$

Here are some other super-sized numbers that I can't even pretend to grasp the quantity of:

Seventillion = $10^3 * 10^3 * 10^{210} + 3$, *or* $10^6 * 10^6 * 10^6 * 10^{45}$

Heptekillion = $10^3 * 10^3 * 10^{51} + 3$

Heptacontillion = $10^3 * 10^{210} + 3$

Heptecillion = $10^3 * 10^{51} + 3$

Septaugintillion = 10^{420}

Thousand-septuagintillion = 10^{423}

Septnonagintillion = 10^{294}

Septoctogintillion = 10^{264}

Septseptuagintillion = 10^{234}

Septuagintillion = 10^{213}

Septsexagintillion = 10^{204}

Septenquinquagintillion = 10^{174}

Thousand-septenvigintillion = 10^{165}

Septenvigintillion = 10^{162}

Septenquadragintillion = 10^{144}

Septentrigintillion = 10^{114}

Thousand-septendecillion = 10^{105}

Septendecillion = 10^{102}

Septenvigintillion = 10^{84}

Septendecillion = 10^{54}

Thousand-septillion = 10^{45}

Septillion = 10^{24}

Konigsberg's Seven-Bridge Problem

A lot of folks have been having problems with walking and doing math at the same time for some time. The old Prussian town of Konigsberg had lots of bridges, so the big issue for them was to figure out how to find a way to walk across each of the seven bridges spanning the Pregolya River only once and be able to end up where they started. (And we were just wondering where those crazy Prussians are today, weren't we?)

Thankfully, the problem was solved in the eighteenth century by the Swiss mathematician Leonhard Euler (Do we love him or what?—born in 1707 and died on *Sept*ember 7.) He explained, in a nice way, that it is impossible. And there is no truth to the rumor that, because his answer was never accepted, he died of apoplexy.

Seven Sisters Schools

This is as good a time as any to talk for a minute about these colleges. In 1927, in an effort to further promote the higher education of women, a group of all-female colleges was organized. They were Barnard College in New York City; Bryn Mawr College in Bryn Mawr, Pennsylvania; Mount Holyoke College in South Hadley, Massachusetts; Radcliffe College in Cambridge, Massachusetts; Smith College in Northampton, Massachusetts; Vassar College in Poughkeepsie, New York; and Wellesley College in Wellesley, Massachusetts. It was not until 1978 at all seven schools had female presidents. As famous and prestigious as these schools have been, they did not survive as women's colleges; most of them went co-ed mid-century.

Chapter 2

THE ARTS

WHAT HAS BEEN written, studied, performed, painted, sculpted, built, composed and danced that relates to seven? This Chapter list selections from myriad examples available in the disciplines of literature, movies, plays, fine arts, music and architecture. For books, movies, plays and poetry, titles have been chosen that reflect a variety of times; one book from 120 BCE and another from the current best seller list and more from the years between. How long has this seven use been going on? Evidently, using the number seven is neither just an old idea nor one that has lost its appeal.

BOOKS AND OTHER WRITINGS

AS WE HAVE already seen, sometimes people just *like* using the number seven. It has also come to be apparent that septomaniacs also like to list their seven things. These folks fit into one of two groups: either they like to list all the seven things they can think of, or, when they make a list of something, they use only seven examples. Check out the nonfiction section of your local bookstore, library, or the Internet; you'll be surprised how many titles begin with "Seven Ways . . ." or "Seven Things . . .", or "The Seven Most . . ."

If asked, will authors admit there may actually be *eight* ways? For the most part, the seven whatevers are the only ones that count. That's their story and they're sticking to it. It's okay by me—I don't want to mess with these people. They get testy.

Here is what Matthew Hutson said about this in *The 7 Laws of Magical Thinking: How Irrational Beliefs Keep Us Happy, Healthy, and Sane*:

The number seven also holds significance across many cultures, and despite there being seven deadly sins, seven is somehow lucky. The attentive reader will notice that I have defined seven laws of magic for this book. Conceivably, I could have divvied the research into six or eight laws. Did I pick seven for logical, aesthetic, or superstitious reasons? Or merely as a cheap marketing ploy? I suppose the world will never know.

I did want the world to know, so asked him. It turns out that Hutson is not testy at all, and emailed that "In the book I offer four potential motivations for settling on seven laws, and I think all of them apply. Seven also seemed a natural choice because the number has such strong associations with superstition and this is, after all, a book about superstition."

Andy Borowitz, writing in Forbes magazine in May 2003, also noticed this use of "seven" in book titles. The article, titled *The Seven Habits of Highly Effective Self-Help Authors*, says: Habit #1: Get the Number Seven in the Title. "If someone is desperate enough to turn to a mass-market book for answers, nothing closes the deal like seeing the number seven in the title."

Habit #7: If You Have Only Six Habits, Come Up with One More. "It is absolutely imperative that you make up one more, regardless of whether it's helpful or not. Otherwise, you'll never get the number seven into your book's title, and you can kiss the bestsellers list goodbye." So besides being an award-winning funny dude, he's also very observant.

Let's take a short look at some of these writings. I wish I could tell you that I have seven feet of books with *seven* in the title, but I actually have more than thirteen feet of them. Here are just a few samples from my personal collection, chosen from different times, places, and genres:

Seven Years in Tibet, Heinrich Harrer, 1953, Putnam; nonfiction.
Never explaining why, Harrer, an Austrian mountaineer, had been imprisoned by the British but escaped into the Himalayas and spent the next seven years there. Serendipitously, he met and was befriended by the then-teenaged Dalai Lama. What were the seven years, you politely ask? They were 1942–1950. (When Harrer was ninety, the Dalai Lama presented him with the International Campaign for Tibet's Light of Truth Award.)

In the Valley of 7 Cities, Stanley G. Sturges, M.D. 1965, Review and Herald; nonfiction.

In the same part of the world and only a few years later, Sturges, a medical doctor, his wife and children spent several years as missionaries in Nepal. The Sturges family was members of the Seventh-day Adventist church; he brought medical care to the seven villages in the park just over the hill from Katmandu—Banepa, Panauati, Nala, Khadpu, Chaucot, Sanga, and Dhulikhel.

***The Seven Storey Mountain*,** Thomas Merton, 1948, Harcourt, Brace; nonfiction.

Merton tells how he came to be a monk. The title is a bit of a stretch. I had to read the thing more than once to figure out what relevance the seven storey mountain had with anything. But I am fairly certain now that it is a reference to Dante, which Merton was reading as a teenager, and in some translations, Dante mentions a seven-tiered mountain in Purgatory. But even Merton calls it a seven-*circled* mountain in his book.

***Seven Against Thebes*,** Aeschylus.

Okay, so he wrote this in like 467 B.C., and in Greek, but it is a classic, so has been translated a bunch of times and is still available, although not too often in scroll-form. (You can even download it for free from the Internet, http://www.5000freebooks.com/books/summary-AESC_SE.htm.) As you will find elsewhere in this book (the one you're reading, not Aeschylus's), it is the story of old Oedipus and his quest for a successor to the throne.

***Seven Pillars of Wisdom: A Triumph*,** T. E. Lawrence, 1926, private printing; 1935, London Jonathan Cape; nonfiction.

Lawrence ("of Arabia" fame) related the Arab revolt against ruling Ottomans during the World War I era and his involvement. The book is recommended by the likes of Winston Churchill and George Bernard Shaw. With good reason: It is not only an adventure tale, it offers great insights into the Arab people, desert warfare tactics, and has his personal dissertations on human integrity and philosophy. By the way, the pillars have nothing to do with architectural columns, but rather he means pillar in the sense of a fundamental principle.

The Seven that were Hanged, Leonid Andreyev, 1908; fiction.

The Russian lawyer, court reporter, political prisoner and finally, author, penned this novel of impending death from the view of seven people about to die. The doomed are two women and three men—guilty of revolutionary conspiracy against the state—a thief and a murderer. Following their time from sentencing to execution, Andreyev gives insightful observations of human reactions to mortality.

The Siberian Seven, John Pollock, 1979, Word Books; nonfiction.

This is the story of how and why two Russian families are being prosecuted for their Christian faith. Their current dilemma? If they leave the confinement of the American embassy in Moscow, the government will arrest them, and they cannot seek asylum in another country because Russia will not grant them exit visas. John Pollock also wrote ***The Cambridge Seven***.

Seven Gothic Tales, Karen Blixen (a.k.a. Isak Dinesen), Modern Library, 1934; fiction.

If you don't recognize either of the author's names, or the title of this book, you will certainly remember *Out of Africa*, which she wrote just a few years later.

The Jewel of Seven Stars, Bram Stoker, Tor Classics, 1903; fiction.

From the famed author of *Dracula* comes this vengeful-mummy story set in Egypt: the jewel of seven stars has been found, then was stolen from the mummy's death-clutch, so now she's mad and out for revenge. In 1998, this story was made into a made-for-TV movie called *Bram Stoker's The Legend of the Mummy*, starring Lou Gossett, Jr.

The Seventh Moon, Marius Gabriel, 1999, Bantam Books; fiction.

If you like *The Bonesetter's Daughter*, you'll like this book, too. You may read more about our country's participation in the Southeast Asian conflict than you really want to believe, but it's a good read.

Seven Little Sisters Who Live on the Round Ball that Floats in the Air, Jane Andrews, 1861, Ticknor and Fields; juvenile fiction.

You can read it online, http://digital.library.upenn.edu/women/andrews/sisters/sisters.html.

Summer for Seven, Janet Lambert, 1952, Grosset and Dunlap; juvenile fiction.

One of the fifty-five books written by this popular author, this is from the Dria Meredith story line. It has been recently republished by Image Cascade Publishing.

Seven Days in May, Fletcher Knebel and Charles W. Bailey II, 1962, Harper & Row; fiction.

It's beyond me how two men can write a book together, but these guys got it all figured out. This book is a great read, and I bet it'll make a great movie one of these days. Hold the phone! Someone else thought so too – see the movie section below.

Seven Days in June, Howard Fast, 1994, Carol Publishing Group; fiction.

This fictionalized account of the battle of Bunker Hill was written by the author of *Spartacus*, and is one of the seven novels he has written about the Revolutionary War.

AT SIXES AND SEVENS

"But time will not permit: all is uneven, and everything is *left at six and seven*." This quote from *Richard II* by William Shakespeare, inspired several other authors. Or perhaps he himself was inspired by the old adage, or perhaps by Proverbs 1:11 "set all at six and seven." Or by Chaucer: Troilus and Cressida "Set all on six and seven." Or...well, you get the idea—it's not a new idea. Following is a short list of some writings titled Sixes and Sevens:

Sixes and Sevens, O. Henry, 1911, Doubleday, Page; fiction.

At Sixes and Sevens, Maia Pedersen, 1969, World Publishing; nonfiction.

Sixes and Sevens, John Yeoman, 1988, Macmillan; juvenile nonfiction.

Sixes and Sevens, Esther Carlson, 1960, Holt, Rinehart and Winston; fiction.

Sixes and Sevens, Edgar Fawcett, 1881, Doubleday; poetry.

The Seven Dials, Agatha Christie, 1929, William Collins Sons & Co; fiction.

What are the seven dials? (See the section on geography later in the book, unless for some reason you already familiar with the seediest section of London. And if you are, I won't ask why.) In this case, the question should be "what *is* the Seven Dials?" It is a nightclub fronting a secret society.

The Seven Stairs, Stuart Brent, 1962, Houghton Mifflin Company; nonfiction.

Again, you should ask, "what *is* the Seven Stairs" rather than what *are* they. It is the name of a small bookshop in Chicago opened by the author as a young man. Funny thing is, he admits right away that the entrance to the door actually had eight steps instead of seven. The book tends to be preachy about the demise of American reading and writing, and is loaded with name-dropping – but the story still drew me in.

Seven River West, Edward Hoagland, 1986, Simon & Schuster, Summit Books; fiction.

Cowboys and Indians, circus performers and gold miners, railroad tycoons, love interests and big bears—not necessarily in that order, but you get them all in this book.

One Saint and Seven Sinners, Ennen Reaves Hall, 1959, Thomas Y. Crowell Publishers; nonfiction.

This is a collection of stories of a traveling Baptist minister at the turn of (the last) century.

Seven from Heaven, Kenny and Bobbi McCaughey, 1998, Thomas Nelson, nonfiction.

Before learning the classic lesson of "don't mess with Mother Nature," this couple in Iowa conceived and successfully bore seven babies—septuplets—in 1997. Regarding their bounty as God's gift, they found that it does indeed take a village to raise children. The four boys and three girls are Kenneth, Nathan, Alexis, Brandon, Natalie and Joel and Kelsey.

Seven Spells to Sunday, Andre Norton and Phyllis Miller, 1980, published by the authors and good for them (first editions are selling for $75.00); juvenile fiction.

Two kids living in a foster home find an old mailbox that has mysterious gifts delivered to them.

The Seventh Game, Roger Kahn, 1982, New American Library; fiction.

It's the seventh game of the World Series and the games are tied, 3-3, with each having been won by a single run. Oh, the drama.

Seven Wild Sisters, Charles de Lint, 2002, Subterranean Press; juvenile fiction.

The seven girls, Adie, Laurel, Bess, Sarah Jane, Elsie, Ruth, and Grace, get caught in a fairy fight.

Seven Men and Two Others, Max Beerbohm, 1919, Oxford Press; fiction.

Illustrated by the author with his wonderful caricatures, this is a witty and wise fictional biography. Available free online.

Seven Men Who Rule the World from the Grave, Dave Breese, 1990, Moody; nonfiction.

Who were the baddest of the bads—ever? Darwin, Marx, Wellhausen, Dewey, Freud, Keynes, and Kierkegaard. Interesting.

The Seven Lady Godivas, Dr. Seuss, 1939, Random House; fiction.

One of his first, and one of his few, books written and illustrated by Seuss for adults. Hang on to your original copy—it's worth enough to buy seven boxes of Godiva chocolates.

The House of the Seven Gables, Nathaniel Hawthorne, 1851, A.L. Burt; fiction.

If you missed this one on your high school required reading list, you can read the book online for free, at http://www.americanliterature.com/SG/HOSGINDX.HTML. It was made into a movie released in 1941 starring Vincent Price. And, yes, there really is a house with seven gables, at 54 Turner Street in Salem, Massachusetts—and it's open for tours.

The House of Seven Mabels, Jane Churchill, 2002, Avon Books; fiction.

Two besties find a decorating job that comes with a body in the basement.

Seven Summits, Dick Bass and Frank Wells, 1986, Warner Books; nonfiction.

Neither man had seen fifty for a few years, but they did have money and determination and were determined to spend the lot of it to become the first to stand atop the highest mountain on each of the seven continents. (See *Seven Summits* in Geography for the list.)

The 7 Habits of Highly Effective People: Powerful Lessons in Personal Change, Dr. Stephen Covey, 1990, Simon & Schuster; self-help.

Selling well over ten million copies, Covey built an industry on the concepts defined in this self-help book—selling videos, calendars, CDs, tapes, giving lectures and seminars, and publishing sequels.

The seven habits? 1) Be proactive, 2) begin with the end in mind, 3) put first things first, 4) think win/win, 5) seek first to understand . . . then to be understood, 6) synergize, and 7) sharpen the saw.

A book such as this is fodder for parody, and *Seven Years of Highly Defective People, Scott Adam's Guided Tour of the Evolution of Dilbert* steps up to the plate. Actually, to be fair, Adams only borrows from Covey's title.

The 7 Secrets of Financial Success, Jack B. Root & Douglas L Mortensen, 1996, Irwin Professional Publishing; nonfiction.

Although the authors offer nothing new to anyone who has read more than one get-rich manual, this one is pretty—the charts and graphs and insets and even the table of contents are in vivid color with no two schemes the same. If you only buy one such book, this is as good as they come. The seven principles are: Set Goals, Pay Yourself First, Harness the Power of Time, Diversify Your Investments, Manage Your Credit Wisely, Safeguard Your Future, and Seek Professional Guidance.

The Stuff Americans are Made of: The Seven Cultural Forces that Define Americans-A New Framework for Quality, Productivity and Profitability, Joshua Hammond, James Morrison (no relation to the one of the Doors) and Josh Hammond, 1996, Hungry Minds; nonfiction.

We Seven, Virgil I. Grissom, M. Scott Carpenter, L. Gordon Cooper, Jr., John H. Glenn, Jr., Walter M. Schirra, Jr., Alan B. Shepard, Jr., and Donald K. Slayton, 1962, Simon & Schuster; nonfiction.

From the cockpit of the Friendship 7 (see chapter 6 on History), Glenn and the others tell the world their story of becoming America's heroes of the space race. Out of print for over thirty-five years, if you still have your copy, it's going for fifty dollars, although I found mine for two.

Seven Came Through, Captain Edward V. (Eddie) Rickenbacker, 1943, Doubleday; nonfiction.

The ace World War I pilot has been sent on a secret fact-finding mission to US airbases during the Second World War. But as luck would have it, good tail winds and bad navigation sent his transport plane into the depths of the South Pacific. Despite being in his fifties and in recovery from *another* plane crash, Rickenbacker managed to save himself and six other crew members stranded on a raft for more than three weeks. He then resumed his secret duties, wrote the secret reports, and wrote and published this book all well before the end of the war.

The Seven Last Years, Carol Balizet, 1978, Chosen Books; fiction.

When a meteor hits Cyprus, a chain of earthquakes and floods circle the Earth. Thousands are dead, but thousands more just disappear in a flash of radiant light. Is this the last seven years of human existence foretold in the book of Revelation? You won't be finding out, but it's a good read for a Sunday afternoon.

The Seven Minutes, by Irving Wallace, 1969

The Seven Minutes, by J. J. Jadway, Etoile Press

Two different books with the same title? Well, not exactly. In 1977 Irving Wallace (and a couple other people plus a world of list-lovers) wrote *The Book of Lists*, and one of his lists is "10 Memorable Books that Never Existed." Here is what was said about it: "This 171-page most-banned novel in history was a figment of novelist Irving Wallace's imagination in his real book, also called *The Seven Minutes*. The contents of the nonexistent book, according to Wallace, consisted of 'the thoughts in one woman's head during seven minutes of copulation with an unnamed man.'"

In 1986, Irving Wallace wrote *The Seventh Secret*, which has no relevance to the previous book or to quickies, book-banning, or sexual morality.

Just another note on the Book of Lists: in that first edition, there are only about a dozen lists of seven, but they are so odd it makes you wonder what's up. For example:

* ✳ Seven famous men who were full-time or part-time virgins

* ✳ Seven famous body parts

* ✳ Willy Ley's seven future wonders of the world

* ✳ Coals to Newcastle: seven great British export sales, and

* ✳ The authors' seven thoughts for you, the reader.

✳

Sometimes there actually *are* books that share the same title. Two I particularly like are William Empson's *Seven Types of Ambiguity* and

Elliot Perlman's *Seven Types of Ambiguity*. Both of these books are great, but Perlman's is terrific and Empson's is tough.

✳

The Seventh Enemy, The Human Factor in the Global Crises, Ronald Higgins, 1978, McGraw-Hill; nonfiction.

Higgins opines there are seven threats to our future: overpopulation, famine, resource shortage, environmental degradation, nuclear abuse, technologies out of control and lastly, "the human factor—inertia of political institutions and personal blindness to realities." Read it and weep.

Seven Leagues to Paradise, Richard Tregaskis, 1948, Doubleday; nonfiction.

You have time, money, and a book to write, so you go on a journey around the world to find the very best place on earth to spend your time, your money, and write responses to the millions of people who want to do what you did. Where is this Eden? Where is the perfect place? What balance did he find of good economy, beautiful and friendly natives, cosmopolitan accruements and culture, ideal climate, easy transportation? If a league is equal to three miles, and you start in New York, where did he find his paradise? And what was he referencing in "seven leagues"? Your guess is as good as mine, and I've read this thing more than once. And that was hard—it's not at all PC by today's standards, nor did it specifically define his criteria of Paradise, and his reflections don't have much to do with how things are today, so don't waste your time trying to find this missive.

Books about Number Seven

What about all the books, like this one, that are *about* the number seven? I have found five written in the last fifty years:

Eerie Seven: Number of Mystery was self-published in 1971 (Vantage Press) by the author Dorothy Chapman. In her book she lists 57 articles about different "Sevens," including the last chapter, titled "Seven Other Noted Sevens." While, of course, I was anxious to read this book, I sadly didn't find much information I had not already found and documented from other sources.

Seven, The Number of Creation was penned by Desmond Varley in 1976 and published by G. Bell & Sons in London. With much more in-depth research and the inclusion of graphics, graphs, and illustrations, it is focused and authoritative.

Seven Occurrence of Seven in Religion, Mythology, Science, & History. 2003, 1stBooks, nonfiction. In 2003 Margaret Manning also self-published a 108-page book about the occurrences of the number seven in the titled disciplines. I found just enough misinformation for me to question some of the other content, but overall, it's good stuff.

7 The Magical, Amazing and Popular Number Seven, David Eastis, 2007, Aventine Press, nonfiction. OMG. This is another book I wanted to love. Let's face it—our book has a whole boatload of trivia, but hopefully not as trivial as the fact the Oprah Winfrey's grandmother's last name has seven letters or that in the movie *Roxanne* there was a line about the "seven Banana Brothers." The last, and seventh, chapter is titled "Chapter 7 of 7 Seven Sells."

7 The Number for Happiness, Love, and Success by Jacqueline Leo, 2009, Hatchette Books; nonfiction. I really don't know what to make of this book – I had looked forward to its publication since the publishing contract was announced. There are, astoundingly, seven chapters. Reportedly a "media guru", the author is cute and credentialed, but, after a half dozen readings, I still don't grasp how to "use" the number seven to gain the happiness, love, or success. But I do like her use of the Oxford comma.

So there you have my short list of "seven" books. When I first started this research, I found literally thousands of book titles containing the word seven. Barns and Nobel lists 45,172 titles with keyword "seven." Figuring this was probably the most used number in book titles, I did searches on all the other numbers from one to twelve. Sadly, I was wrong. But strangely enough, seven is the *seventh* most-used number in books. So I'm still happy.

Seven Commandments

Animal Farm by George Orwell recounted the happenings when the barnyard livestock usurped the land from the farmer. Establishing a government and laws was one of the first steps they took. Here are the seven commandments as they were *originally* posted:

* ✳ Whatever goes upon two legs is an enemy.

* ✳ Whatever goes upon four legs, or has wings, is a friend.

* ✳ No animal shall wear clothes.

* ✳ No animal shall sleep in a bed.

* ✳ No animal shall drink alcohol.

* ✳ No animal shall kill any other animal.

* ✳ All animals are equal.

Authors' use of Seven

Sometimes it happens that the number seven inadvertently just keeps popping up in a book and the author is probably not even aware of it. Take *The Firm* by John Grisham. The second half of the book is especially rife with sevens; in one nine-page sequence, Grisham mentions seven nine times. He talks about "seven years," "the seventh floor," "seven files," "the seven button," Seven Mile Beach, and uses seven copiously in telephone numbers. Grisham's take on that? He is silent. The rest of the book continues using seven, but, hey, I have a life and am not about to go counting such things for too much longer.

Some authors, though, use seven deliberately. Read the introduction to the 1986 publication of *A Clockwork Orange*. Almost twenty-five years after the book first appeared, author Anthony Burgess is still miffed that the last chapter had been omitted from US editions. He wrote the original manuscript in three sections of seven chapters each, saying "Novelists . . . are interested in what is called arithmology, meaning that number has to mean something in human terms when they handle it. The number of chapters is never entirely arbitrary." He liked the omitted seventh chapter of section three, but was cold and hungry at the time, and the publishers sent him an advance, so . . .

Here is a quote from the back-cover of *Where the Heart Is*, by Billie Letts and selected to Oprah's Book Club:

> *Talk about unlucky sevens. An hour ago, seventeen-year-old, seven months pregnant Novalee Nation was heading for California with her boyfriend. Now she finds herself stranded at a Wal-Mart in Sequoya, Oklahoma, with just $7.77 in change.*

Mrs. Number Seven is a character in book 5 of the Harry Potter series. But alas, her name isn't really Mrs. Seven. She lives at house number 7, across the street from Harry's aunt and uncle. Perhaps they forgot her name.

PERIODICALS

Seven Soldiers of Victory

Back in the 1940s, DC Comics had a company called National Periodicals in need of new group of superheroes, comprised of members already established in their own strips who would band together to vanquish the foe of the week. Here's the line-up: the Shining Knight, Green Arrow, Speedy, the Vigilante, the Star-Spangled Kid, Stripesy, and the Crimson Avenger. Together, they saved the world from 1941 through 1945.

Sovereign Seven

From 1995 to 1997, Chris Claremont and Dwayne Turner pumped out thirty-six issues using visitors from the planet Meridian as superheroes. They are: Cascade (a.k.a. Rhian Douglas), Cruiser (a.k.a. Nicholas Hellicon), Finale (a.k.a. Pahe Leilani Fava'ela), Indigo (a.k.a. Conal Savoy), Network (a.k.a. Taryn Haldane), Rampart (a.k.a. Jaffar ibn Haroun al-Rashid), and Reflex (a.k.a. Walter Thorrson.)

The Seven Guys of Justice

A satirical spoofy goof on other comic book gangs of superheroes, published by False Idol Studios, we think located in Beaverton, Oregon. Brian Joines is the creator-writer genius behind the series. Originally the seven were: The Surprise, Lord Talon, Johnny Explode, Hunter-Gatherer, Nightie Knight, Ugly Monkey and Moray Earl.

Seven Years of Highly Defective People, Scott Adam's Guided Tour of the Evolution of Dilbert.

We, the office workers of America, have loved Dilbert, and we loved this compilation of cartoons. Scott Adams made it more than just a reprint of his favorites by adding commentary.

The Seven Sisters of women's magazines

For several decades now, periodicals purveying pithy platitudes of wisdom to those of us wending our way towards the ideals of feminine pulchritude and the practice of domestic wiles—sorry, I got carried away for a moment—have been known as the Seven Sisters. They are: *Better Homes and Gardens, Family Circle, Good Housekeeping, Women's Day, Ladies' Home Journal, McCall's,* and *Redbook.* The earliest reference to "seven sisters" is back in the 1950s and is characterized as a trade-designation. Recently these seven have been suffering from an aging readership and competition from start-up successes such as *O!,* and *Martha Stewart Living.* But for crying out loud, they have all had a good run – these magazines were all established between 1876 and 1932, and as of 1998, the lowest Folio 500 Rank among them was number thirty-four.

MOVIES

MOTION PICTURES ARE known as "the seventh art," a term coined by Italian film pioneers Ricciotto Canudo and Louis Delluc in 1916, or 1911, depending on what source you believe. The other six arts are: architecture, sculpture, painting, music, dance, and poetry.

The Seven Per-cent Solution, 1976.

Directed by Herbert Ross. Check out this cast: Alan Arkin, Vanessa Redgrave, Robert Duvall, Nicol Williamson, Laurence Olivier, and Joel Grey. The Academy Awards nominated Nicholas Meyer for best adapted screenplay (from his own book) and also Alan Barrett for best costumes. The title refers to the dosage of cocaine used by Sherlock Holmes (in the Doyle books.) Here, Doctor Watson and Sigmund Freud help him the cure his habit, while Holmes, of course, solves a crime.

The Seven Year Itch, 1955.

Directed by Billy Wilder. Starring Marilyn Monroe and Tom Ewell (who won the Golden Globe Best Actor for his role.) The screenplay was adapted by George Axelrod from his own play. It is a social satire about man's urge to roam from marital straights in the seventh year of wedlock. It is famous of course for the scene where Marilyn's white halter dress is blown waist high.

Seven Sinners, 1940.

Directed by Tay Garnett (who had a cameo appearance as a drunken sailor; Garnett also directed Cinerama's *Seven Wonders of the World* in 1956). As a sultry singer in a South Seas cabaret named the Seven Sinners, Marlene Dietrich attracts men like lonely seamen to a busty broad. Oops—guess there is no metaphor there. One of them is a young John Wayne.

The Seven Minutes, 1971.

Directed by Russ Meyer. Adapted from Irving Wallace's novel of the same name, this semi-successful movie starred John Carradine, Alexander D'Arcy, Yvonne de Carlo, Tom Selleck, Jackie Gayle, and Wolfman Jack.

Se7en, 1995.

Directed by David Fincher. Starring ("the hottie") Brad Pitt, Morgan Freeman, Gwyneth Paltrow, and Kevin Spacey. A creative killer continues his quest to clean up the world —one sinner at a time. See Religion for the list of seven sins. See the movie for the one sin you never can remember.

Seven Years in Tibet, 1997.

Directed by Jean-Jacques Annaud. Starring ("the hottie") Brad Pitt and really no one else that anyone remembers. The Dalai Lama as a young person, however, was portrayed just as we would hope the once and future god-man would have been at that age.

Sinbad: Legend of the Seven Seas, 2003.

Brad Pitt ("the hottie"), Catherine Zeta-Jones and Michelle Pfeiffer lend their voices to the sailor's animated adventure.

Seven Days in May, 1964.

Directed by John Frankenheimer, screenplay by Rod Serling, starring Burt Lancaster, Kirk Douglas, Fredric March, Ava Gardner, Edmond O'Brien, and introducing John Houseman. Epitomizing the Cold War paranoia, with espionage, kidnapping, murder, and distrust. There's self-doubt in the West Wing, loose lips in the Pentagon, low morale in the military ranks, affairs and pseudo affairs, big guns and big egos . . . a guy movie from the get-go.

Six Days, Seven Nights, 1998.

Directed by Ivan Reitman. Stars Harrison Ford, Anne Heche, and David Schwimmer (of TV's *Friends*) and Allison Janney (of TV's *West Wing.*) If you want a fun and funny romantic comedy, here it is.

Seven Samurai, 1954.

Directed by Akira Kurosawa. Starring more than seven Japanese actors with whom we were unfamiliar in the West, didn't even recognize half a century ago, and didn't care. A small village is tired of the bandits taking their profits so hire a group of questionable toughies to take care of them. It's old, it's long, it's foreign with subtitles, and it's a winner. We loved it so much, it was remade by Hollywood as:

The Magnificent Seven, 1960.

Produced and directed by John Sturges. The seven samurai are cast as seven Mexican bandito-banishers: Charles Bronson, Steve McQueen, Robert Vaughan, James Coburn, Brad Dexter, Yul Brenner, and Eli Wallach, who plays the bad guy. The story is the same, only the country and language have been changed. We won't try to examine why all the Mexicans speak English. Besides this no-loser cast, the music we all know from the Marlboro commercials (when cigarette companies were allowed to advertise on TV). There was a 1966 sequel, *The Return of the Magnificent Seven*.

Seven Men from Now, 1956.

Directed by Budd Boetticher, starring Randolph Scott, Gail Russell, and Lee Marvin. This was the first of seven movies director Boetticher and Scott made together. The plot is a little blurry, as are the characters—there are bad guys doing good deeds and good guys being really bad. We eventually learn our hero is on a quest to kill off the seven men who hauled off and killed his wife. Not to mention they hauled off a boatload of his gold.

Snow White and the Seven Dwarfs, 1937.

A Walt Disney production made by a handful of directors. As Disney's, and the world's, first full-length animation project, it is a masterpiece of color, character, and charm. They were able to take the fairy tale and clean it up for modern children by omitting the blood and guts and adding music and warmth. The seven dwarfs were named Bashful, Sneezy, Sleepy, Happy, Grumpy, Dopey and Doc. Walt Disney received a special Academy Award, which was a full-sized Oscar statue and seven miniature Oscars. The award was presented to him by Shirley Temple.

The Seven Little Foys, 1955.

Directed by Melville Shavelson. Bob Hope stars as Foy in the musical biography of the vaudevillian trouper. The "seven" are his seven children he takes on the road with him.

Seven Road Movies

Bob Hope and Bing Crosby made seven *Road* pictures together:

* ✳ *Road to Singapore* (1940)

* ✳ *Road to Zanzibar* (1941)

* ✳ *Road to Morocco* (1942)

* ✳ *Road to Utopia* (1946)

* ✳ *Road to Rio* (1947)

* ✳ *Road to Bali* (1952)

* ✳ *Road to Hong Kong* (1962)

Seven Brides for Seven Brothers, 1954.

Directed by Stanley Donen. Screenwriter Albert Hackett adapted this musical comedy from Vincent Benet's book *Sobbin' Women*, which was based on the Greek legend of the Sabine women (just a little play on words there.) In all the stories, the men were wishing to, but forbidden from marrying their chosen women, so choose to kidnap them – but for keepers rather than ransom.

7 Faces of Dr. Lao, 1964.

Directed and produced by George Pal, starring Tony Randall and Barbara Eden. Adapted by Ben Hecht from the book *The Circus of Dr. Lao* by Charles Finney.

A "stranger comes into town and helps everyone become better people" story. Why seven faces? Because Dr. Lao has some sort of traveling circus and Tony Randall plays seven of the different characters.

Robin and the 7 Hoods, 1964.

Directed by Gordon Douglas. Frank Sinatra, Dean Martin, Bing Crosby, Sammy Davis Jr., Peter Falk, Barbara Rush, Edward G. Robinson, and Victor Buono lead the cast in this musical comedy. For a couple hours we watch the Rat Pack playing Chicago gangsters laundering money by making charitable donations.

Seven Chances, 1925.

Produced, directed and starring Buster Keaton. The scenario: You can inherit $7 million dollars if you marry by seven p.m. Hmmmm. Can he pull this off? One would think so, especially after witnessing the currently popular reality shows that offer substantially less of a challenge. The prologue is in two-strip Technicolor—amazing for 1925.

Seven Beauties, 1976.

Directed by Lina Wertmuller. Pasqualino, played by Giancarlo Gianini, has seven, well, let's say "unlovely" sisters, one of whom is abused by a pimp, who is then butchered by Pasqualino for his efforts. A second story in the story is about his life in a German prison camp during World War II. "Seven Beauties" is Pasqualino's nickname.

Seven Alone, 1974.

Directed by Earl Bellamy. Set in 1843 on a wagon train from Missouri to Oregon, this true story tells of the Sager family seven children, who made the trip alone after their parents died.

Woman Times Seven, 1967.

Directed by Vittorio de Sica. This is a series of seven short vignettes starring Shirley MacLaine:

* As Paulette in *Funeral Procession*

* As Maria Teresa in *Amateur Night*

✳ As Linda in *Two Against One*

✳ As Edith in *Super Simone*

✳ As Eve in *At the Opera*

✳ As Marie in *The Suicides*, and

✳ As Jeanne in *Snow*.

Bunk alert! You may hear on the internet rumor mill that the Academy Awards' Oscar weighs seven pounds. Don't believe everything you hear.

PLAYS

Morning's at Seven, Paul Osborn.

The title of this multi-Tony-winning 1939 play was taken from a line in the drama-poem "Pippa Passes," by Robert Browning. The original cast included Dorothy Gish (my dear grandmama's second cousin, thank you very much) but the show ran for only forty-four performances. The 1980 revival in the same theater had better luck, with 564 performances and three Tony winners (David Rounds for Featured Role, Vivian Matalon for Director, and the play itself for Best Reproduction.) In 2002, the play again was well-received and was awarded nine Tony nominations. Estelle Parsons received a nomination for Best Actress, and you'll see her name again a little later. The 2002 reproduction had an outstanding cast, including William Biff McGuire, Stephen Tobolowsky, Nancy Marchand, and Maureen O'Sullivan.

The comedy concerns four sisters living in a small Midwest town, giving us a view of two days in their existence. It is shot-through with platitudes, stigmas and trite family dynamics and lacks a strong plot line, but somehow the characters carry it off.

Seven Descents of Myrtle, Tennessee Williams.

Obviously not one of Williams' better efforts, this drama involves the triangle between two brothers and one's wife each in a ploy to receive an inheritance of a plot of land, which doesn't seem worth the effort as it is on a flood plain of the Mississippi River and the waters are rising. As Williams had a wont to do, this play began life as a short story in Esquire magazine in 1967, then morphed into a two-act play. It was rewritten and renamed and revised several times along the way to its timely and fortunate demise.

Estelle Parsons won a Tony nomination for this play in 1969, despite the fact that it ran for only twenty-nine performances. Jo Meilziner did the set design, which he also did for *The Seventh Trumpet* in 1941 and *Morning's at Seven* in 1939. Jane Greenwood did the costumes for this production, and also for *The Seven Descents of Myrtle* in 1968.

Gore Vidal thought it a worthy enough effort to try it as a movie. Retitled *Blood Kin: The Last of the Mobile Hot-Shots,* it didn't do much better on the silver screen than on the boards of Broadway, even with his cast of James Coburn, Lynn Redgrave, and Robert Hooks. It received an R rating and lousy reviews.

The Seven Year Itch, George Axelrod.

Presented on stage in 1953, Tom Ewell was cast as our hapless, fantasizing leading man, a role for which he won Best Dramatic Actor Tony. And did so without the help of Marilyn Monroe.

Seven Brides for Seven Brothers, Albert Hackett, Frances Goodrich, and Dorothy Kingsley. This play received a Tony nomination in 1983 for Best Score, music and lyrics by a combination of Gene de Paul, Al Kasha, Joel Hirschhorn, and Johnny Mercer.

Seven Guitars, August Wilson.

Seven Guitars is the story of a Pittsburgh blues singer who goes to Chicago in 1948 to record two songs. After he returns to Pittsburgh, he is jailed for 90 days on a phony charge. When he gets out, he discovers that his record is getting airplay and he is asked to come back to Chicago to make additional records. However, he is killed before he can go, and the play is told in flashback after his death. The song that is played to signify his hit is "Who's Loving You Tonight?"

Ruben Santiago-Hudson's Tony for acting was the only winner, but the play received seven other nominations in 1996. It also was nominated for a Pulitzer Prize for drama in 1995.

The Lie Direct

When William Shakespeare (1564-1616) wrote *As You Like It*, TouchStone enumerated seven classifications of lies (act 5, scene 4):

* ✳ The retort courteous

* ✳ The quip modest

* ✳ The reply churlish

* ✳ The reproof valiant

* ✳ Counter check quarrelsome

* ✳ The lie with circumstance

* ✳ The lie direct

DANCE

Noverre's Seven

Back in the late 1700s, Jean-Georges Noverre, known as "the Shakespeare of the dance," analyzed all the movements of ballet dancing. He reduced them all to just seven: bend, stretch, rise, leap, dart, glide, and turn. Of course, being French, he gave all the movements classy French terms (*plier, e'tendre, relever, sauter, e'lancer, glisser,* and *tourner*) that still serve today as the basic terminology for this dance.

TELEVISION

7th Heaven

This WB series ran eleven seasons. The premise of the soapy family-oriented drama: a handsome young minister and his beautiful supportive wife bring up their seven charming children in a loving and intelligent way, despite all the trials and tribulations of life. When the writers can get through all that without being schmaltzy, bully for them. Evidently they did well, as the show was widely acclaimed and awarded. Starring Stephen Collins and Catherine Hicks as the parents, the seven children were: David Gallagher (Simon), Beverly Mitchell (Lucy), Mackenzie Rosman (Ruthie), Jessica Biel (Mary), Barry Watson (Matt), and the twins, who, since children of that age must have twins to play a role, must be played by two sets of twins and they are not given credits.

Seven

Seven was a short-lived character on *Married with Children* in its seventh season. For reasons only the writers can explain, they thought he would be a nice addition to the show's cast. Viewers thought otherwise, and Seven, played by Shane Sweet in the 1992-93 season, who had appeared from out of the blue, just as quickly faded into the gray.

"Seven"

"Seven" was an episode in the seventh season of *Seinfeld* (2/1/1996). George Costanza tells his fiancée Susan that he wants to name their future kid Seven, he says to honor Mickey Mantle. No one seems to share his enthusiasm, except Susan's cousin, who used the name for *their* new baby.

Seven of Nine

Seven of Nine was a character on *Star Trek: Voyager*. Annika Hansen, a tot of six years old, along with her researching parental figures, crashed on a moon. It is thought she was the first human to be assimilated as a Borg. As an adult, she has made her way to the starship, and though she lacks social graces, she finds a home and job. Played by Jeri Ryan, somehow the character became one of the more popular ones on the series. You may not remember her, but she is the gal with the butch haircut and the glob of stuff that may be scar tissue hanging off her left eyebrow. Maybe that thing got on her eye when she was busy infiltrating someone else's left cerebral hemisphere with a nanoprobe.

Seven Words You Can Never Say on Television

In 1972 comedian George Carlin joyfully enumerated seven words that were considered obscene and were to be avoided during on-air radio and television broadcasts. Reportedly, a single man called the station to report his objection, since his teenaged son heard the list. This ultimately led to FCC v. Pacifica Foundation, a 1978 United States Supreme Court trial that resulted in a set time for "dirty" words to be broadcast during the hours when youngsters were probably in bed. The court, in this very narrow decision, also granted the FCC wide leniency to determine exactly what words were obscene. Carlin's list sometimes changed the seven words and they won't be listed here but can be readily found.

The Seven Ages of Man

Some themes are simply just appealing, and are used and reused throughout the world and time. Here is an example:

William Shakespeare around 1599 wrote a famous soliloquy spoken by Jaques in *As You Like It*, Act 2, Scene 7. You'll recognize the beginning:

All the world's a stage,
And all the men and women merely players;
And one man in his time plays many parts,
His acts being seven ages.

Here's Shakespeare's list:

* The infant, mewling and puking in the nurse's arms.

* The whining school-boy . . . creeping like a snail unwillingly to school.

* The lover, sighing like a furnace.

* Then a soldier, full of strange oaths . . . seeking the bubble reputation even in the cannon's mouth.

* The justice . . . full of wise saws and modern instances.

* The sixth age shifts into the lean and slipper'd pantaloon, with spectacles on nose and pouch on side . . . pipes and whistles in his sound and then:

* Last scene of all . . . is second childishness and mere oblivion, sans teeth, sans eyes, sans taste, sans everything.

Anonymous:
* Spills

* Drills

* Thrills

* Bills

* Ills

* Pills

* Wills

Bill Cosby lists these "ages" in his 1988 book *Time Flies*:
* Preschooler

* Pepsi generation

* Baby boomer

* Mid-lifer

* Empty nester

* Senior citizen

* Organ donor [15]

Crosby Gaige wrote a delightfully witty book in 1941 (if you ever get a chance to read it, you will not be sorry. Anyone who can make a cocktail guide funny . . .) called *A Vous*. He cleverly suggests "the feminine palate . . . brought the cocktail out of its swaddling clothes into this present vast wardrobe of drink." The following is from chapter 9, "The Seven Ages of Women":

* Baby's Breath (1/2 jigger mild, ½ jigger prune juice, dash of Paregoric)

* The Sub Deb (1/2 French Vermouth, ½ Italian Vermouth)

* The Debutante (1 ½ jigger of gin, lime juice, Crème de Menthe, Angostura bitters)

* The Wedding March (1 jiggers White rum, lime juice, 2 egg whites, Angostura bitters)

* Papa Loves Mama (1 part Kirsch to 3 parts dry white wine; "pour till it hurts")

* The Black Widow (2 parts dry gin, 1 part apricot brandy, 1 part orange juice)

* The Dowager Duchess (this one's rather involved, as is life at this time) [16]

Ogden Nash, the wonderfully popular poet, on staff at and often quoted in *The New Yorker*, got into the act of seven in his 1933 poem "The Seven Spiritual Ages of Mrs. Marmaduke Moore." Same theme, but enumerated as only Nash could do.

Chhit-ji-a

In Taiwanese, there is a particular form of poetry called Chhit-ji-a, that has seven syllables in each verse. Literally translated, the word means "that which has seven syllables." Those clever folks!

MUSIC

SHALL WE NOW discuss music theory? It'll be painless, I promise. Think about an octave—eight notes on the scale we normally use. It's really only seven unique notes, isn't it? A, B, C, D, E, F, and G. So why would a music scale be divided into seven notes?

Because I couldn't get all this figured out all by myself, I asked for an explanation from a really smart musician, Joseph Meyer, who has a way of "explaining things so that I can understand them."

He says: "The octave actually refers to the interval from 1 to 1, for example from middle C to the C above it. So while there are only seven different pitch classes (A's, B's, C's, etc.) we count from 1 to 7 and then one more to 8 to form an octave. For all practical harmonic purposes 1 and 8 are the same, in this case both being C."

And what is a seventh? More from Joseph: "Now a seventh is actually the interval from the first to the seventh note of a scale, in this case from C to the B above it. Matters are complicated somewhat by the use of the minor and other scales, which differ from the intervals we hear when we play only the white keys on a piano from C to C. You may have noticed that you have to throw in some black keys to play major scales that do not go from C to C, because of the uneven distribution of whole and half steps in a scale. On a piano keyboard there are alternating groups of two and three black keys. The distance between any two adjacent keys is a half-step, so the white keys that have a black key between them are a whole step apart, and those without are a half step apart. A major scale is all whole steps, except between steps 3 and 4, and steps 7 and 8. Minor, diminished, and other assorted scales are configured differently."

And how did all this come into being? Why aren't there six notes, or fifteen, or ten?

"The Western scale is derived from something called the overtone sequence, which has its basis in physics. When a string vibrates, it vibrates not only as a whole, but in segments which produce overtones. Overtones are not only that which gives particular instruments their character and music its warmth and beauty—without them it would all sound like computer beeps—they are also how scales are derived. If you touch a string in the exact center as it is vibrating, it will kill the main pitch and leave only the overtone one octave higher, also known as a harmonic. It had been producing that pitch all along, but it was not something that was obvious to the ear when the main pitch was sounding. Other pitches, like the fifth one up, are derived similarly, from portions of the string that are vibrating independently as it sounds."

Oh, but there's more: "Unfortunately, if you derive a scale this way and then derive scales from each of the pitches thus produced, you end up with a whole bunch of slightly different pitches. The way this was dealt with in Western music was through something called the tempered scale, which tweaks each of the pitches slightly to produce a compromise. This allows one to play anything in any key without retuning. (Bach's *Well-Tempered Clavier* was an early exploration of this scale.)"

Anything else, Joseph? "A *seventh* is also a term used to refer to a chord consisting of the first, third, fifth, and seventh notes of a scale."

MUSIC TERMS WITH SEVEN

Leading Tone (or leading-note)

This is a major seventh of any scale, the semi-tone below the keynote.

Septet

A composition of either seven instruments or seven singers.

7tt

This is the abbreviation for "septet."

Subtonic

Literally translated, this means "under tone." It is the seventh tone of a diatonic scale.

Pelog

Gamelan is a term from Indonesia for a percussion music ensemble. Literally it means "things struck together." The struck things are like gongs, drums, bells, cymbals, and metallophones. The musicians play long, intricate performances without the aid of written music or a conductor. Gamelans are thought to have come from the Hindu gods and may go back as far as the third century BCE.

Andrew Timar, a Canadian composer and instructor, explains "Pelog is a 7-tone hemitonic tuning system (this scale has semitones.) In the Pelog family of scales, a number of 5-tone modes are used, which can be considered sub-sets of the possible 7 tones within the octave." [17] All clear?

Hexachord

Back in the eleventh century, an Italian named Guido of Arezzo, who really needed meaning in his life, developed a theory in music about hexachords. I'm going to quote Madeleine Ladell, an English editor who explains this theory.

In medieval music, a succession of six pitches, separated by the intervallic distance tone, tone, semitone, tone, tone, that forms the basis of the Guidonean system of solmization. Guido proposed that if seven hexachords are overlapped at particular intervals, the resulting range . . . and organization of pitches may be used as a device for indicating the intervals required to sing plainchant. If a melody extends beyond the range of a given hexachord, the hexachord in use is said to "mutate" . . . in order to accommodate the new note(s). [18]

So there. Overlapping intervals, required devises, mutating notes—this all sounds rather scary to me, so let's be glad we don't hear too much medieval music while we're driving.

Music of the Spheres, a.k.a. musica mundane

Earlier I talked about how the ancients believed there were seven "spheres," or visible heavenly bodies. Pythagoras went so far as to believe that each one of these planets also emitted a musical tone—the tone being determined by the planet's spinning speed and distance from the earth—and the seven tones formed a scale. It was conceded that we humans could not actually *hear* this music, but even so, it's there nonetheless and its power rules our world.

MUSICAL INSTRUMENTS

Seven-String Guitars

Judging from all the internet discussions on the subject, there has been a lot of interest in this model. Invented by Andreas Sichra (1772-1861) in Russia, the instrument "has an additional bass string, tuned one fourth below the standard tuning." Ibanez is the most popular current manufacturer of the seven-string guitar, and because many nu-metal bands (like Deftones, Korn, and Limp Bizkit) use them, their popularity has risen recently.

Kora

Many nations in West Africa use an instrument called a kora, which has a half-circular gourd bowl with a wooden neck. Twenty-one strings placed in two rows. These strings symbolize a family, with seven strings belonging to the mother, seven to the father, and seven to the child.

Ngoni

Also from Western Africa is a lute called the ngoni. It has only seven strings and is small but has a big sound. It has an animal skin stretched over the hollow wood body, so it's almost like a drum but for those strings.

Wasa Wombe

I'll tell you about one more African instrument. The wasa wombe is made from an L-shaped stick. They attach seven calabash disks to this by drilling a hole in their centers. So what you end up with is a shaker-thing that sounds like maracas or castanets.

Grammy Winners

2002—Best Historical Album: *Louis Armstrong: The Complete Hot Five and Hot Seven Recordings*, performed by Louis Armstrong. The award was won by Phil Schaap, Seth Foster, Tom Ruff and Woody Portpitaksuk, who were the mastering engineers.

1998—Best Mexican-American/Tejano Music Performance: *Los Super Seven*, performed by Los Super Seven: Joe Ely, Freddy Fender, David Hidalgo, Flaco Jimenez, Ruben Ramos, Cesar Rosas, and Rick Trevino.

1965—Best Classical Vocal Performance: *Salome (Dance of the Seven Veils*, by Richard Strauss and performed by Leontyne Price.

Dance of the Seven Veils

This opera, written in 1905 by Richard Strauss, was inspired by Oscar Wilde's play *Salome*, a relatively new hit stage at the time. Strauss expanded on a misguided notion that Salome (who is never named in the Bible as the notorious dancing girl) did a strip-tease before King Herodias, her uncle and mom's new husband, and as a reward was presented John the Baptist's head on a plate. It was scandalous when first performed.

Sevens, by Garth Brooks

I don't know what to do with this information, but in 1997 Garth Brooks released his seventh album. It contains seven tracks per tape side. The first 777,777 copies of the CD are marked as "first editions," making them collectable.

7, by Enrique Iglesias

Released in 2003, Iglesias either wrote or co-wrote all of the songs on this album, which was his seventh.

Beethoven's Seventh Symphony

First conceived in 1808, Beethoven finally finished his seventh symphony in 1812. It was first performed in the University Hall in Vienna as a fund-raiser for the Austrian and Bavarian armies in their war against Napoleon. And although some critics at the time regaled it as his finest effort to that time, and tell us the audience insisted on the allegretto being repeated, others were more critical, saying nasty things like, "he is quite ripe for the madhouse," and "it's like a lot of yaks jumping about."

ARCHITECTURE

Seven Wonders of the World

Let's jump right in to the most famous of the lists of seven: the Seven Wonders of the World. Why are there seven wonders? Congratulations! That is one of the FAQs that can only be explained by the number seven being so embedded in the tradition, history, and mythology of Middle Eastern culture that no other count would have even been considered. The first reference to the concept can be found in the writings of Herodotus in 500 BCE, the Fodor's of the day. Initially compiled as a travel guide for that century's jetsetters (or camel-sitters), these were the seven must-see places to visit in ancient times. They probably still would be but were already ancient when the list was compiled, and only one remains today. All were creative engineering marvels:

* The Great Pyramid of Khufu (aka Cheops), Giza, Egypt. Until the 1800, this 450-foot- high structure was the tallest building on earth, a record that held for about 4,500 years. The base, a square 756 feet on each side, is aligned with the compass, and chambers and passageways found within mimic several

astrological paths, leading to all kinds of theories as to the pyramid's true use. Was it more than a pharaoh's tomb? Constructed of massive mined blocks of stone, it is beyond comprehension how the thing was erected.

* The Hanging Gardens of Babylon. King Nebuchadnezzar is credited with the erection of the gardens, reportedly as a way to bring some homeland flora into the life of his young bride, Amyitis. It was no easy task to reconstruct a forested mountain in the middle of Mesopotamia—beside the need for planters large enough to hold full grown trees, the logistics of getting water to the top was compounded by erosion when the water flowed back down. So we must assume that rock and bricks formed the terraces, but nothing remains to verify this except the descriptions that were already ancient in biblical times.

* Statue of Zeus. Back when the Olympic games were first held, say in 776 BCE, the grand Pooh-Bah of the Greek gods was Zeus. With all the contestants and tourists pouring into Olympia every four years, it was of course necessary to erect impressive facilities and monuments to make the trip memorable to them all. In 456 BCE a temple was built in honor of Zeus, but after a few years it was considered too simple, so Phidias was commissioned to do a statue to reside within its walls. He designed a seated Zeus forty feet tall and twenty feet wide, which pretty much filled the interior space. Phidias began with a wooden frame and covered it with ivory, gold leaf, ebony, and gems. Maintenance was a nightmare due to the extremely dry climate, but that issue was dealt with effectively until 392 CE by which time, Christianity had decided that sporting events were rather pagan, and the monument was in grave danger of being destroyed. Some Greeks with deep pockets had the statue moved to Constantinople (a city built on seven hills) for safe-keeping. All went well for seventy years, then a fire destroyed the monument.

* The Temple of Artemis. This temple, probably the last in a long series built to honor Artemis (or Diana, as she was also known) was commissioned to Scopas of Paros in about 356 BCE. Pliny, the Roman historian, reports the building was 425 feet by 225 feet and the gently-sloping roof was supported by 127 columns. He tells us it took 120 years to construct, but that's disputable. Alexander the Great happened upon the construction in 333 BCE and offered to finance its completion, but the city officials of Ephesus, in a very tactful way, declined his offer and finished the job without his fundage. A large souvenir market prospered around the shrine and was instrumental in keeping the burgeoning Christian faction from destroying the source of their livelihood for several centuries. By 262 BCE however, the efforts failed. Building stones were used for other local construction projects and the temple dismantled into oblivion. Pieces can be viewed today in the British Museum and a single column has been re-erected at Ephesus to commemorate the original location.

* The Mausoleum at Halicarnassus. Here is yet another great love story. This city and surrounding lands were ruled by Mausolus who died in 353 BCE. His widow-sister, Artemisia, heartbroken and understanding his love of Greek architecture, decided to erect the most elaborate tomb to date. Knowing the reputation of Scopas (see above), he was sent for and authorized to erect the structure. A site overlooking the city was procured and the courtyard designed upon a platform. Sculptured lions flanked a staircase to the top of the platform. A marble square rose from the center, tapering to a 140-foot-high pitched roof. The tomb was supported by thirty-six columns sporting a statue between each one. The roof was adorned by massive sculpted horses pulling a chariot ridden by Mausolus and Artemisia. Within two years of her husband's death, Artemisia succumbed to the inevitable, and was also interred within. For seventeen centuries the mausoleum stood in the hills above the city, when, in the half-cen-

tury before Christ, a series of earthquakes shattered the site. Later came the Crusaders, who used the marble for their own construction and recycled the stone for castle-fortification. What remains today is a seven-foot chariot wheel from the roof sculpture, which can be viewed at the British Museum in London.

* The Colossus of Rhodes. Likened to the Statue of Liberty because of its similar stature and symbolism, the Colossus of Rhodes was erected as a monument to freedom. Located on the island of Rhodes at the point where the Aegean Sea meets the Mediterranean, the city had been under siege of the troops of Demetrius for an extended period and wished to commemorate their ultimate victory with a gigantic statue of their patron god, Helios. They used the enemy's siege tower as the scaffolding and melted the bronze from the war machines to clad the statue. At 110 feet tall, the nude, crowned icon stood shading his eyes with his right hand on the east and held a cloak in his left.

* The Great Lighthouse at Alexandria. It was erected in about 290 BCE in Egypt. The city of Alexandria had been busy creating itself as a harbor of both the Nile and of the Mediterranean Sea. Lacking neon and needing something to guide the trade ships into the harbor, the ruler Ptolemy asked Sostratus of Knidos to build the world's first lighthouse on the island of Pharos. The building was marble blocks with lead placed between the joints—this probably about 200 feet high and 100 feet square. Topping this section was an eight-sided tower topped by a cylinder topped by an open cupola lighted by an open fire and graced with a statue of Poseidon. A large mirror projected the fire's light over the water. The locals loved the attraction, which became a tourist draw. Alas, it was again Mother Nature who devised its demise, in earthquakes in 365 and 1303. Perhaps the final fall was in 1326, which would date its lifespan at almost 1,500 years.

The Seven Lamps of Architecture, a 200-page 1849 essay by John Ruskin.

Taking his bride on a European honeymoon, John Ruskin penned this treatise on what he defined as the basis for classic architecture—sacrifice, truth, power, beauty, life, memory, and obedience. Divided into seven chapters, the "lamps" have nothing to do with lighting fixtures but are lamps as in a source of knowledge. Surprisingly, it became a best-seller.

Temple of the Seven Dolls, Dzibilchaltun, Yucatan.

The Mayans built this structure about 1,500 years ago. It has a ninety-five-foot square base, is almost fifty feet high, has a series of tiered stone steps on all four sides leading up to the entrances, is made of stone and stucco, and remarkably, still stands. The unique feature of the temple is that it is the only one erected with windows and a tower. It is a simple structure having a single central chamber and surrounding corridor. Above the east entrance is an altar adorned with hieroglyphics. Here, seven figurines, or dolls, were placed as offerings.

Seven Mile Bridge, Marathon, Florida.

Originally constructed in 1912 as a railway bridge, it was reconstructed between 1979 and 1982 as a girder, or hollow-box external prestressing bridge for automobile traffic, replacing several others then existing. It has 440 spans and is the largest segmental bridge in the world. Its superstructure and piers are formed from precast, prestressed concrete, which in December 2002 was found to have more deterioration than expected. It is now listed with the National Register of Historic Places and can still be walked across. A new bridge has been constructed alongside, but it is only 6.79 miles and was completed in 1982.

Vysotniye Zdaniye (Stalin's Seven Skyscrapers), Moscow

After many of Moscow's major buildings were demolished during the reconstruction of the 1930s, Stalin embarked upon a grandiose plan to erect a series of gigantic skyscrapers. World War II delayed the construction until the 1950s, when he commissioned these buildings to be erected in a ring around central Moscow. Eight were planned, but only seven completed: the Ministry of Foreign Affairs, the Hotel Ukraine, the Moscow State University Tower, Kotelnicheskaya Naberzhnaya, Kudrinskaya Square, Leningradskaya Hotel, and the Red Gate Square. All were tiered neo-gothic structures with central towers, in the wedding cake style. After one had been given a glass and metal spire, Stalin liked the look so well he had similar spires added to the others. The buildings are often referred to as the Seven Sisters (how original).

Seven World Trade Center, New York

Completed in 1985 by architectural firm Emery Roth & Sons as part of the World Trade Center, this office building was the baby of the block, standing only forty-seven stories. On September 11, 2001, at 8:45 in the morning, a hijacked airliner crashed into One World Trade Center. At 9:03, another hijacked passenger jet embedded itself into Two World Trade Center. At 4:10 that afternoon, Seven World Trade Center began burning. An hour and ten minutes later, it collapsed into the pile of rubble along with the other six buildings of the World Trade Center.

Temples

Buddhist temples have seven main buildings: the to (a pagoda), a kondo (the main hall), a kodo (where lectures are held), a shoro (a bell tower), a kyozo (the sutra depository), a sobo (the dormitory where monks live), and a jikido (where the monks eat.) The layouts differ, but usually the pagoda is the main building and is placed in the center.

Prince Shotoku, esteemed as the father of Japanese Buddhism (brought to Japan from Korea and China—the religion, not the man), is credited with the erection of the **Seven Great Temples of Nara**, constructed in India at the start of the seventh century. They are: Daianji, Gangoji, Horyuji, Kofukuji, Saidaiji, Todaiji, and Yakushihi.

Chapter 3

COMMERCE AND RECREATION

L ET'S EXPLORE NOW the ways in which some well-known – and lesser-known – companies use the number seven in their names, logos, and on their products. We'll get the inside scoop from some of them about why they do this. Have you wondered what the 7 in 7UP means? Why are pencils seven inches long and 45 rpm records seven inches in diameter? Why did the telephone company decide to use seven digit telephone numbers (not all countries do, you know)? John Elway, craps, water polo. What do they all have in common? If you cannot guess by now, you have probably opened the book to a random page – which by the way, is just fine to do. Let's mix some business with pleasure. . .

Companies and Their Products

I have written, emailed, and called scads of companies that have "seven" in their names, asking them why they did that. After confirming that this was one of the oddest questions they had received to date, most of them said it is just because seven is lucky or has good connotations. People are always surprising, aren't they? I was *expecting* them to say it was because they had seven founders, or the office was located at 7 West Jersey Street, or they began with seven products—and some of them did. Following are just a few selected "seven" companies—and I realize that I am omitting a few. Thousand.

Will the real Seven jeans please stand up?

So. You're young and rich and so chic that dressing up means wearing designer jeans. The ones to be seen in are Sevens—but are you getting the real deal? Gerard Guez started Seven Licensing Company and bought the US rights to use the name Seven7. These rights were purchased from the French entrepreneur Maurice Ohayon, who had owned the name worldwide since 1998, a label first trademarked in Italy in 1978. In 2002, Seven Licensing Company filed a suit against L'Koral, who was manufacturing jeans using the label Seven. L'Koral had filed a suit several months earlier against *them*, saying their name did not in fact, infringe on Seven7. And their jeans are actually 7 for all Mankind. L'Koral is owned by Michael Glasser and Peter Koral, who reportedly use the name as an honorarium to a former gig at Lucky Brand Jeans and Glasser's baby, who was born July 17, 1987 and weighed in at seven pounds and seven ounces.

Nippon Tabako Sangyo

For Japan's largest purveyor of cigarettes, the brands **Mild Seven** and **Seven Stars** are the sales leaders. Privatized by the Japanese government in 1985, this corporation employs 16,000 people and has thirty-one cigarette factories across their nation. Seeking to expand their sales across the world, the company ran into problems in Europe and Canada with Mild Sevens—it seems it is illegal there to use the word *mild* in a cigarette name. They are still working out the issue. This could be a crucial thing, as Mild Seven is the world's second largest-selling brand and holds a 34 percent market share in Japan. (Seven Stars had 7.7 percent of the share as of 1999.) Here's a funny: If you purchase a pack of these cigarettes *in Japan*, the words "Seven Stars" and "Mild Seven" are written in English. I think that's odd.

7UP

Mr. C. L. Grigg is the genius behind this icon of soft-drink brand names. He is my hero. He was not a young man back in the early 1920s when he took his lifetime knowledge of marketing and advertising skills to found his own company. His first—and only—product then was Howdy Orange drink, but he spent a lot of time testing and developing a new flavor from lemons and limes. Finally, he found the perfect taste and brought it to market—in October 1929. Oops. There he was, with a new product just a couple weeks before the stock market crashed. Making matters worse, he named it "Bib-label Lithiated Lemon-Lime Soda" and charged more for it than the competition, and the competition was more than 600 other similar drinks. Being the savvy marketing man he was, he soon changed the name to 7UP, which didn't hurt his already popular drink. By the late 1940s 7UP was the third largest selling soft drink on earth. That's quite a tribute to marketing.

So why the name? There aren't too many people who can keep a secret, but old Mr. Grigg was one who could, and the knowledge died with him. Sorta makes you wonder what the big deal was—and what else he wasn't telling. The folks still there at 7UP have a really fun website (but are very snarky about letting me use their name.) They offer several rumors that are going around but generously say "just make 7UP yours and tell your own story." Which I would, but now that you know it's not true.

Actually, the trademarked name was purchased from a Minnesota candy company that made chocolate candy bars with seven different fillings. [19]

Jack Daniel's Old № 7

Here's another product with a seven that no one knows the reason for: Jack Daniel's Old No. 7. And again, the company has a fun website and some good-humored folks as employees. Maybe they are all taste-testers. John and my friends at Jack Daniel's patiently explained to me that a *lot* of people ask them about the origin of the name.

"Fact is, though, no one really knows what it refers to," says John. "It's just something that Mr. Jack Daniel started calling his Tennessee Whiskey, but there are no written records stating why." John says there are a lot of rumors, but he's not going to spread them around.

Seagram's 7 Crown

"In 1934 the 7 Crown Distilling Company introduced . . . 7 Crown. The crown-topped "7" first appeared in advertising in November 1946." [20]"...Founders aged, a second generation of brand builders appeared on the scene, accelerating the introduction of new products, new brands, and truly changing and improving the face of the supplier tier of the industry. Most noteworthy was Victor Fischel of Seagram who introduced 5 Crown and 7 Crown." [21] By 1942, production of 5 Crown was halted so they could "concentrate" on the 7 Crown.

If you ask for a "seven and seven", you'll get Seagram's 7 mixed with 7UP.

Platinum 7X Vodka

This vodka is distilled by an old company established in 1969, Sazerac, in Metairie, Louisiana. The vodka is made from only the best corn and is distilled—wait for it—seven times.

Seven Oaks

Jerry Lohr was one of the first to dare begin a winery in the central coast of California in the 1960s. In the early 1970s, he planted the original 280 acres of grapes in Monterey County and in San Luis Obispo County by 1986. The company now tends to almost 3,000 acres of vines. One of their unique, "green" campaigns now is to recycle the corks.

Seven Daughters

This company cellars and bottles both red and white wines from King City, California. The seven that are blended on the bottle I have are Syrah, merlot, Zinfandel, Carignane, Sangiovese, cabernet Frauc, and cabernet sauvignon.

Seven Sisters

There really are seven sisters behind this brand of wine! They live and work in Paternoster, on the African cape's west coast. They obtain their grapes from the vineyards in the Swartland area. Each of the seven sisters has a wine named for her: Bukettraube for Odelia, Pinotage Rose for Twena, Chenin Blanc for Yolanda, Sauvignon Blanc is Vivian, Pinotage/Shiraz is Dawn's, Merlot is June's, and the Cabernet is for Carol.

Seven

Seven is a red table wine from Spain. I found mine in a three-liter octagonal box that says I have reduced the packaging by 92 percent and carbon emissions by 55 percent. So yeah!

Seven Hills Winery, Walla Walla, Washington

Founded in 1988 by Casey McClellan and company, this newcomer has already won several prestigious awards for its reds. And no wonder—we are told the Mr. McClellan has a master's degree in wine yeast performance, and if that won't do it . . .

The wines are in limited production and not nationally distributed, but if you can get your hands on a bottle of the Cabernet Sauvignon 2002, you won't be sorry. Be warned, though: the wine contains sulfites. If the government thinks it is important for us to know that, I want to be sure to pass the information along to you fellow consumers.

7 Deadly Zins

The Michael~David Vineyards in Lodi, California, bottles a zinfandel they call 7 Deadly Zins. Even the bottle is lots of fun—a clever front label which incorporates the numeral 7 into the Z in *Zins*, and the back label has poem naming not only the seven sins, but also the Lodi vintners from whence come the grapes. Or blackberries. Or cherries. At twenty dollars a bottle, is it greed or pride?

You'll also find bottles of Michael~David's 7 Heavenly Chards nearby—another cute label and poem. They advise us that this Chardonnay has been "aged in barrels from seven different French coopers."

That may be a bit of a stretch to get in the seven-connection, but they are so nice about it all and seem to have so much fun with the business, that we'll let it go.

Guinness

Seven percent of the Irish barley crop is used in the production of Guinness beer. Just a fun fact to know and share. Actually, this statistic is from several years ago but is repeated so many times on various websites that if I didn't include it somewhere in this book, someone would be writing me.

7X

Here's another corporate secret: the flavoring mixture of Coca-Cola. It is known as 7X. This all got started back when Asa Candler bought the rights to the Coca-Cola formula. By that time, quite a few folks already knew the secret formula, so he changed it. But he still had high hopes of keeping his *new* recipe *really* secret, so he had all the labels removed from the ingredients and coded even the orders for supplies and their invoices. The codes were just numbers, all except for the flavoring recipe, which he called 7X. Alas, the secret finally did get out and has been published in several books and on the Internet. The earliest written document with the recipe lists ingredients and flavoring separately, so the flavoring had its own recipe, which was a combination of the following seven ingredients:

80 Oil Orange	40 Oil Nutmeg	40 Oil Cinnamon	40 Oil Neroli
120 Oil Lemon	1 Qt. Alcohol	20 Oil Coriander	

Nabisco's Ritz crackers

What's up with people who know stuff and won't share? There are seven holes in a Ritz cracker. Why? Well, it seems that the good people at Nabisco weren't *about* to tell us. They said it's a matter of corporate security. They are sure we will understand. Being a persistent cuss, I tried again. Here is the second response: "As much as we'd like to assist you, the information you're requesting isn't currently available. We apologize for any disappointment this may cause." [22]

Do you think if we *all* starting asking about the seven holes and letting them know just how deep our disappointment really is that they would change their minds and tell us?

The Seven-Course Meal

We often hear "from soup to nuts" as an expression of something being start to finish. This comes from the old tradition of having a seven course meal. Peggy Post in the sixteenth edition of *Emily Post's Etiquette* says that the seven courses are soup, fruit, fish, entrée, salad, dessert and coffee. (Where are the nuts?) But she is not the only authority. Amy Vanderbilt's *New Complete Book of Etiquette*, published twenty-five years before Peggy Post's book, says they are in fact soup, seafood, entrée, salad, dessert, petits fours, and demitasse. (Again, where are the nuts?) As a matter of fact, Miss Manners (Judith Martin) is really, truly the only one who really knows and is up-to-date. And she opines that the meal should actually be 14 courses. But of course, the first is soup and the last is nuts.

7-Eleven

Are you working at a firm that takes employee suggestions and innovations seriously? An enterprising dock worker of the Southland Ice Company in Dallas was. He started selling bread, milk, and eggs to folks coming in for ice, and did okay at it. So pretty soon the company built a whole store right there on the warehouse dock and kept it open sixteen hours a day—from seven a.m. to eleven p.m. That was back in 1927, which made 2002 the company's seventy-fifth year of operation, and, clever folks that they are, July 11 (7/11, see?) was declared the official birthday.

Today, 7-Eleven is the world's largest convenience store retailer, with more than 39,000 locations. Being industry leaders along with the ability to change their product lines and target market has put them in that position. They were the first to remain open twenty-four hours a day (but did not change the name to 24-7, as we might have expected), the first to serve coffee to go, the first to advertise on national television, and the first to let customers serve themselves at the soda fountain. They also sold us the first thirty-two-ounce Big Gulp—hey, thanks—and since we were still thirsty, they up-sized to the sixty-four-ounce Double Gulp. That's four pounds of liquid, friends and neighbors—how do we do it? Especially with no in-store public restrooms. But the thirst goes on, so they sell us the most cold beer, bottled water, and Gatorade of any retailer, plus a million cups of coffee a day, and 11.6 million Slurpees and almost 3.5 million gallons of milk every month. And still no public restrooms.

"I was a seven-stone weakling."

This is the way the English heard the Charles Atlas body-building advertising, while we Americans were being told "I was a ninety-seven-pound weakling."

A stone equals 13.85 pounds.

Seven Sisters oil companies

Now I'm just guessing with this one, but I bet there is someone out there in the world who thought they were quite clever when they dubbed the seven big oil companies the Seven Sisters. Maybe they even thought it was original and catchy. The seven were Exxon, Royal Dutch/Shell, Texaco, Gulf, Mobil, BP, and SoCal.

Well, not really. Standard Oil of New Jersey was once Exxon after it was Esso. Standard Oil of New York morphed into Mobil Oil then merged with Exxon and ExxonMobil was born. What I called BP began as British Anglo-Persian Oil Company before it was British Petroleum and before their merger with Amoco (American Oil Company, which used to be Standard Oil of Indiana, which of course was the mighty Standard Oil before the government broke it up) and became BPAmoco. It's now just referred to as British Petroleum – or just BP. Again. Standard Oil of California (SoCal) was once Chevron before it was ChevronTexaco. This explains what happened to Texaco. Chevron also consumed a big chunk of Gulf Oil. But these big boys are still known as the Seven Sisters. Go figure. And isn't ConocoPhillips now in the list?

Seven Sisters film studios

Many referred to the original seven Hollywood movie studios as the Seven Sisters:

* Columbia

* Disney

* Fox

* MGM

* Paramount

* Universal

* Warner Bros.

IBM and the Seven Dwarfs

Once upon a time, there were many corporations competing in the mainframe industry. One, IBM, was a very large and powerful player. The others (Burroughs, Control Data, General Electric, Honeywell, National Cash Register, RCA, and Univac) were dwarfed by her large size. Some of the little guys, like General Electric and RCA, didn't play in this game for very long—they had other games to play anyway. Honeywell was eaten by a French Bull. Burroughs and Univac got married. NCR went to live with AT&T for a few years. Control Data took their ball and went home. We all miss those little dwarfs, don't we?

Seven Towns

This is a company in London that will "evaluate and license other peoples (sic) inventions." "We want to create elegantly designed innovative leisure products and through the success of these products create wealth for our clients and ourselves." One of their most famous products is the Rubik's Cube. [14] They are located at 7 Lambton Place, London.

Seven Bank Ltd.

Seven Bank, based in Tokyo, began life as IY Bank. They placed ATMs inside the Japanese 7-Elevens and the Ito Yokado general merchandise stores and functioned as primarily an Internet bank. In 2005 the first brick-and-mortar site was opened. The bank accepts ATM and credit cards, even foreign ones, and processes the transactions to withdraw yen. They also have partnered with Western Union to do international money transfers as part of their service.

Seven Cycles

Biking enthusiasts know this new company well. I mention them here because of the astute reasoning for their name: "At its conception, Seven's founders sought a name that would be as timeless, ageless and positive as the products they would create. Finally, 'Seven' was chosen because it is a time-honored number that holds positive connotations and no specific attachments to other objects. We chose a work, like a product, for which we could set the standard." Hear, hear![23]

And while we are on the subject of cycles, check this out! Staller Studio in the Netherlands manufactures a *tricycle* built for seven riders. The brainchild of renowned artist Eric Staller, this contraption began life as a four-wheeler, but further refinements have brought it down to three motorcycle wheels. They say the thing can make a "U-turn in its own length (240 cm)." The driver-rider sits in the back seat and everyone pedals. Or not, if they wish. The models are available for rent and are being touted as great ice-breakers and team-builders for any event. You can buy one too if you would like.

System SEVEN

This is where you go when you search www.seven.com: "SEVEN enables mobile operators to offer turnkey mobile data access services to their enterprise customers. The company's patented System SEVEN architecture provides secure, manageable, real-time mobile access to enterprise applications from any device and across any network." All that *and* has a zero-footprint. Whew. Sit me down and blow me away. I've been asking around and have found out from some geeky friends that they mean you can now use your cell phone to get all kinds of work done while you are away from work. If any one of you ever shows this product to my boss, I'm going to be coming after you. Seven did, however, provide seven compelling reasons why I would want to work for them. Reason number seven is that Six and Eight are not hiring. And why *Seven*? Meredith Valt, Seven's senior marketing manager told me "...the standard party line as to why we chose the name." She writes, "Seven is a number that is rich in meaning, from the Seven Wonders of the World to the lucky number. Seven also signifies our mission of becoming the next '7' in the telecommunications world. The last 7, Signaling System 7 (SS7), transformed the public switched telephone network by making intelligent network services such as caller ID and call forwarding possible and by enriching the voice offering that mobile operators delivered to their customers. The new Seven will transform the global wireless network by making new data services possible." She adds, "As you can imagine, we've gotten great feedback over the last few years." [24]

Seven Corporate

If you've ever watched TV in Australia, you've run across this company, which owns stations in all the major cities—on channel 7, of course. Beyond that, they also publish magazines, own Telstra Dome (a large sports arena in Melbourne), Ticketmaster7, and a chunk of a mobile telephone company.

Since Company Seven was so kind and honest answering my questions, I'll use them as an example of pragmatic corporate nomenclature. This group says they are in the business of resourcing for "the international professional astronomical, nature watching, and law enforcement/defense communities." They sell telescopes. Hugh O'Neill writes that the company founders were firefighters in Prince George's County, Maryland, working at fire company—as in station—number 7. "We felt no need to learn how to answer the telephone any other way than what we were already used to saying." It's a good thing to know your limitations.

Imus

Some corporations have sevens incorporated in their logos. Imus, a company in the Philippines that makes movies, has seven stars on theirs. Here is their reasoning: "There are seven stars in the logo because Imus Productions was formed in the '70s, and there are seven children of Ramon and Azucena. And the seven rays of the sun, according to Bong." They "represent the tenacity of our production outfit to give our utmost to the industry, seven days a week, inspired by the strength and light of the sun." (Huh?)

Austin Seven

Anyone remember the Austin Seven? This was a cute little inexpensive car developed by Sir Herbert Austin in the early 1920s as an answer to the horsepower tax then in effect in England. It had seven horsepower. The Seven grew along with the economy and by 1937 the engine had 900cc and was dubbed the Big Seven. In 1938, the last Seven rolled off the production line, but the engine continued to be used in small cars until the 1960s, being put into car bodies such as the Reliant. It was also used in airplanes and motorcycles. The body was licensed to be produced by Dixie in Germany, which later became BMW. More than fifty different body designs were sold in their years of production, making the collecting of them a widely varied and interesting hobby, as attested to by the huge number of owners' clubs throughout the world.

Seven-shooter

Any of you older folks remember the TV show *Johnny Ringo*? The hero was famous for carrying a seven-shooter. But alas, Hollywood just invented the gun. (Case Thomas concocted the device after seeing a Confederate pistol of a similar design.) It was purported to be a .45-caliber revolver, with the seventh shot coming from the added-on .410 shotgun barrel. Just the flip of a switch to the firing pin was all it took to do in the last bad guy. Somehow, each week there were six bad guys—until the seventh showed up.

Model Seven MS, Remington

Here is Remington's verbatim description of this gun:

This compact rifle is built around a 20" Custom Shop barrel fitted to the Model Seven action, and bedded in a classic, satin-finished, full-length Mannlicher-style stock. The select hardwoods have been chosen for their clear grain, and pressure laminated for the strength and dimensional stability demanded of this design. The butt stock features a straight comb with raised cheek piece and 1" black rubber recoil pad. . . . The front of the carbine is finished off with a steel Mannlicher-style fore-end cap, and sling swivel studs are supplied fore and aft. [It] is available in twelve short-action calibers. [25]

777-7777

I know this has been a question burning in your brains: Why do we have seven digits in our local telephone numbers? "In the mid-1920s, AT&T instigated a universal system for assigning telephone numbers so that dialing would be possible rather than calling the operator to connect you with your intended party." I would dispute the era this was begun, or else it took several decades to accomplish the task, so I'm going to relate the saga as remembered by Bill Culbertson, whose family actually owned a telephone company and knew what transpired: Ma Bell decided they needed a universal method of assigning unique telephone numbers, so they contacted all the private telephone companies around the country—and at that time there were hundreds—and told them what their local three-digit prefix would be. Ma Bell had no hope that we would be able to remember a seven-digit number, so they told the local companies to find a word they could abbreviate to two letters, which would leave only a word plus five numbers to memorize. For instance, the telephone company in my little home town was assigned the prefix 278, so they were told to find a word beginning with a combination of A, B, or C (letters on the 2) and P, R, or S (letters on the 7). The main street in town was Broadway, so *BR* was chosen. When someone asked our phone number, we would then reply "BRoadway 8-1234." By 1958, we had become sophisticated enough to be able to remember all seven numbers without the need for the abbreviated word. Still, it took more than fifteen years for us to stop *saying* the words and start *saying* the numbers.

And by the way, there is no area code 777. Yet.

Seven-Second Delay

Not knowing exactly what else to call this phenomenon, and not sure if it is accurate, we'll go with what we have: This is the delay between what is broadcast on the radio and when you actually hear it. So when you are talking to a radio personality on the air while you have your radio tuned in to that station—how else would you be able to hear yourself say the wildly witty comments?—you are asked to turn off your radio. Otherwise, what you end up hearing, along with the rest of us, is an annoying echo.

There is also a seven-second delay to purportedly catch profanity and get rid of cranks. Someone is making a good living—we can only hope—by listening to all the call-in comments and DJ discourses and speedily bleeping the bad words before they reach our sheltered, delicate ears. (See: "Seven things you cannot say on the air" for a complete listing of what the courts deemed too raunchy for American listening pleasure.)

Seven-Inch Pencils

Take the eraser and metal eraser-holder-on'er band off a pencil and you will find the wooden part to be seven inches long. That's the industry standard—or at least, it is the industry norm. Henry Petroski, an engineer, professor, and author of *The Pencil: A History of Design and Circumstance*, [26] writes, "In 1934 the Bureau of Standards issued . . . a draft of 'Simplified Practice Recommendation R151-34 for Wood Cased Lead Pencils.' Standard lengths . . . for wood cases . . . were specified . . . [and] the elimination of the six-inch-long pencil was proposed, making the seven-inch standard." But it was never to be officialized, and by 1938 the pencil industry was involved in more serious problems than formalizing an agreement as to how long to make their pencils.

But *why* are pencils seven inches long? Queries to several pencil-making firms resulted in answers like, "We don't know. Go ask Henry Petroski; he wrote the book."

Petroski answers: "My belief is that the pencil's length imitated that of a painter's brush, thus giving it the feel of a brush, which had evolved over a long period of time. The standard pencil length is one that most writers have become comfortable with. It has the right heft and balance. Many writers, me included, find that as a pencil is used and sharpened, its shorter length does not feel right in the hand." [27]

So there you have it—seven inches just feels good. Hoo, Baby, it feels so good.

I should just mention that the folks at the pencil manufacturer Sanford, in an effort to be helpful, told me they produce "more than seven million pencils a day at our plant in Lewisburg, Tennessee." A *day*. Now I don't wish to disparage sales of this company's product, but who on earth is buying all those pencils? And *why*? The pencils I currently own must be separated a fair distance from each other or they tend to breed.

From Pencils to Paper...

A few years ago, on the back of the stall door in the restroom of a favorite local restaurant (I find odd seven-things in some odd places) I read the following trivia: "You cannot fold a piece of paper in half more than seven times." Running back to the table, I tried this with the napkin—and sure enough, I couldn't do it. We started folding all sorts of paper things that happened to be lying around our table until we were politely asked to stop—and to go. Our paper napkins at home must be a cheaper, thinner brand, because we were able to make 8 folds. Ditto on our tissue paper and wrapping paper and Kleenex, but not on the dinner receipt from that restaurant. So there we have it— another myth debunked!

My quest was pretty much satisfied in that single evening, but others have taken the challenge rather more seriously. Britney Gallivan, while still a junior in high school, not only studied the problem and devised mathematical equations for folding in alternate directions *and* folding in a single direction, but also wrote a book about her experience. (*How to Fold Paper in Half Twelve Times – An "Impossible Challenge" Solved and Explained;* $6.00 + tax.)

Seven-Inch 45 RPM Records

On March 31, 1949, RCA Victor introduced their first 45-rpm records. They sold for forty-nine cents (that's seven cents per inch)—inexpensive even way back then—and played for about five and a half minutes on each side. One song on Side A and a second on Side B. Why did RCA choose to manufacture records that were seven inches in diameter? There are several stories, but here's the one that seems to ring true:

> *The 45 rpm speed was the only one to be decided by a precise optimization procedure (by RCA Victory in 1948.) Calculus was used to show that the optimum use of a disc record of constant rotational speed occurs when the innermost-recorded diameter is half the outermost-recorded diameter. That's why a 7-inch single has a label 3½ inches in diameter. Given the CBS vinyl groove dimensions and certain assumptions about the bandwidth and tolerable distortion, a speed of 45 rpm comes out of the formula. [28]*

Bulletins sent to the sales outlets touted the records as being less expensive to purchase, easy to carry and store because of the small size, and easy to identify by their color-coding. The classifications of the music—and there were seven—were coded by the color of the records themselves, not just the labels. The colors were: blues & rhythm —orange; children's music—yellow; classical—red; country & western—green; international— sky blue; popular—black; and popular classical—midnight blue.

They only used the colors until 1952, when all the 45s were black again. So if you have one of those colored puppies, you should hang on to it. *Especially* if yours was included in "The Certain Seven"—those records no dealer could afford not to keep in stock in 1948:

* Forever and a Day by Perry Como

* Riders in the Sky by Vaughn Monroe

* "A" You're Adorable by Perry Como

* Careless Hands by Sammy Kaye

* Don't Rob Another Man's Castle by Eddy Arnold

* Bouquet of Roses by Eddy Arnold, and

* Claire de Lune by Jose Iturbi.

K7

Say "K7." In French this time, s'il vous plaît. A little rusty, are you? Kā set. The French word *cassette* that we use all the time, is abbreviated by them as K7. The Portuguese do this, too – as they phonetically say K7 *cá sete*.

"Magic Number Seven for Decision Making"

This was the title of the BBC News Online article by Helen Briggs in September 2001. She was reporting that a study had been conducted by the University of Glasgow, led by Professor Simon Garrod. The professor and his group concluded that groups larger than seven people had a hard time reaching a decision. They report that groups such as juries, cabinets, and business conferences are ineffective when more than seven people are present. They become more "like monologues, with each speaker broadcasting their view to other participants." They determined that group size is "vital for decision-making." So, if you want a successful, unanimous decision, you had better keep the body count low.

PERSONAL FINANCES

Bankruptcies

When I first sent out a request for information on bankruptcy, I received a barrage of replies from lawyers all over the United States and from as far away as Australia. Leonard G. Leverson, an attorney in Milwaukee, was kind enough to share a lecture he presented to the Milwaukee Bar Association outlining the history of this subject. Titled "Sabbatical, Jubilee, and Release: The Biblical Origins of the Discharge in Bankruptcy and the Status of the Discharge in the Jubilee Year," he outlines in great detail the biblical references that call for the forgiveness of debts on sabbatical years. Sabbatical itself is derived from the Hebrew word meaning seven, and logically it occurs once every seven years. Some references apply to the release of indentured slaves on the seventh year, if the servitude was for debts. Debts themselves were also to be forgiven on the seventh year, but allowances were made if a person volunteered to pay the debt. Other limitations also applied, as when a debt was secured by real estate or by a shopkeeper or if incurred by rapists or compelled by a court.

Today in the United States, a discharge of debts under Chapters 7 and 11 can be obtained by an individual once every seven years. This has been in effect since 1903. Leverson opines that Congress might have had the sabbatical year in mind when they enacted this change.

For more information on bankruptcy, see the chapter 6, "History and Government."

Credit Reporting

There are now three major players in the credit-reporting game. They are the folks who collect all the information about how well and often you pay your credit card bills, and who you have credit cards with and for how long, and who owns your mortgage, and how many people are asking for your credit history, and all the names you've ever used, where you have bank accounts, and holy moly who knows what else about your personal finances. And how long does all this information—good and bad—stay on that report? The kind folks at

TransUnion had this to say, "The time limits . . . apply to federal law, state laws may vary." They go on to list the seven (!) types of reports that remain for seven (!) years on your file: (italics are mine)

* Accounts—Adverse information from your charge accounts can remain for up to *seven years from the date of the first delinquency* on the account.

* Bankruptcy—"A completed (discharged) or dismissed Chapter 13 remains on file for seven years from the date filed. The actual accounts included in bankruptcy remain on file for seven years from the date of closing/last activity regardless of which chapter you filed."

* Civil Judgments—"...remain on file seven years from the date filed *regardless if paid or unpaid.*"

* Tax Liens—"*Paid* tax liens remain on file for seven years from the date *paid.*"

* Foreclosure Public Record—"Foreclosures, both paid and unpaid, remain on file seven years from the date filed."

* Forcible Detainer—"...both paid and unpaid remain on file seven years from the date filed."

* Garnishment and Attachment—"A garnishment and attachment remains on file seven years from the date filed." [29]

In addition, though, *you* may add information that will also stay on the report for seven years. It is a Seven–Year Victim Statement, also known as the FVAD seven-step program. (Because, duh, it, duh, has seven steps, duh, to follow.) When you do this, for the next seven years every time you try to open a charge account at your new favorite store, the store will be told to call you at home before granting any credit. And you are probably standing right in front of the clerk instead of home answering her call, so you'll probably have to wait instead of getting a new account right then and there. This is for folks who are concerned about identity theft and are taking precautions.

Universal Product Codes

A UPC is the barcode that you see on just about all products that are sold. Check out the one on this book's back cover and get out your magnifying glass. It is a scan-able series of black and white bars that represent a 12 digit number. The number uniquely identifies the product and its manufacturer. Actually, even though they identify a product, the description and pricing is not included—it takes a computer to find this information. Each digit consists of a series of seven spaces, or in other words, a combination of seven black bars and white spaces.

Digits are encoded like this:

0 = 3-2-1-1
1 = 2-2-2-1
2 = 2-1-2-2
3 = 1-4-1-1
4 = 1-1-3-2
5 = 1-2-3-1
6 = 1-1-1-4
7 = 1-3-1-2 (bar-space-bar-space)
8 = 1-2-1-3
9 = 3-1-1-2

Because each digit is seven spaces, each encoded number will add up to seven.

SPORTS AND RECREATION

No S

There are currently only seven professional sports teams in the United States that have team names not ending in *s*: the Miami Heat, Orlando Magic, Utah Jazz, Colorado Avalanche, Tampa Bay Lightning, Chicago White Sox, and Boston Red Sox.

Heptathlon

A heptathlon is an athletic contest, usually for women, which has seven events: 200-meter foot race, 800-meter foot race, 100-meter hurdles, shot put, javelin throw, high jump, and long jump. It is sort of an Iron Woman contest. In 1984, the Olympics replaced the pentathlon with the heptathlon. It was won that first year by Glynis Nunn of Australia. Jackie Joyner-Kersee of the United States won the silver. But in 1988 and 1992, she won the gold. She also took the NCAA and US National championships in the 1982-83 season, the World Championship in 1987 and 1993, *seven consecutive* US National heptathlon titles in the years 1990 through 1996, and the Goodwill Games championship in 1991. At the Goodwill Games in Moscow in 1986, she was the first woman to score 7,000 points in a heptathlon.

Wearing the Seven

Athletes, a group of superstitious folks if ever there was one, like the numeral 7 on their jerseys. It seems to bring luck to some of them.

John Elway, formerly of the Denver Broncos and inducted into the Football Hall of Fame in July of 2004.

Kevin Johnson, while playing with the Phoenix Suns. March 7, 2001, the team retired his uniform number 7 during halftime of a game Phoenix played against the Sacramento Kings. Johnson is now mayor of Sacramento, his hometown.

Doug Flutie, Jr. of the San Diego Chargers

Toni Kukoc of the Chicago Bulls, the Philadelphia Sixers, the Seattle SuperSonics, the Milwaukee Bucks, yadadada, has worn the number 7 while playing for all of those teams. And for a bunch of the European teams he played with before he came to the United States.

Joe Theismann—Quarterbacks at Notre Dame were not allowed to wear double-digit numbers on their uniforms, so Joe Theismann was assigned jersey number 7. He had some good college years, so he stuck with the number, wearing it later in the CFL and then with the Redskins in the NFL.

Mickey Mantle—Playing for the New York Yankees, Mantle wore the number 7 for eighteen years. He had seven pinch-hit home runs in that time. My favorite quote of his: *"During my eighteen years I came to bat almost 10,000 times. I struck out about 1,700 times and walked maybe 1,800 times. You figure a ballplayer will average about*

500 at-bats a season. That means I played seven years without ever hitting the ball."

For a more complete listing of athletes wearing seven, go to http://www.basketball-reference.com/friv/numbers.cgi?number=7.

The Seventh-Inning Stretch

Ah, America. We love our traditions and who the hell cares how they began? We love our baseball games, too, but who among us can sit through nine innings? President Taft gave us all permission to take a break when he stood to stretch at a Washington Senator's game in 1910. Being respectful folks, when our chief executive stood, all the other fans did too, and the president established the precedent. At least, that's the story most often told. In reality, the practice has been documented as far back as 1869. Another urban legend busted!

Short Subjects

* Sports with seven team members to a side: water polo, rugby, netball.

* A regulation softball game has seven innings.

* "Seven, no trump" is the highest bid possible in contract bridge.

* Checkers has only seven possible opening moves.

* Mark Spitz won seven gold medals in the 1972 Olympics.

* If you play basketball and are seven feet tall, you are a septipedalian.

* You are dealt seven cards when playing crazy eights.

* Opposite faces of a die always add up to seven.

* There are a maximum of seven races in the America's Cup finals.

✳ The average life of a major league baseball is seven throws.

Craps

It could be that, in America at least, craps is the game responsible for the number seven being associated in the gaming industry with Lady Luck. It is the one number you will see over and over in any gambling casino—on slot machines, on the souvenirs that are sold, on marquees, and on about anything else. Becoming popular after World War II, craps was one of the most often-played games in casinos. It is, of course, played with dice, those remarkable little cubes with one to six dots on each surface. And if I haven't mentioned it before, the numbers are cleverly arranged so that if you add the dots on the up side with those on the opposite side, you will always get seven. That fact is critical to how the game works:

This is an easy game. Toss a pair of dice and add up the total number of dots you see.

Study this chart and memorize the odds of any number being thrown. You can see that with two dice, there are thirty-six different combinations of numbers and that the most common combination is 7. There are six different ways to throw a 7: 1 and 6, 2 and 5, 3 and 4, 4 and 3, 5 and 2, and 1 and 6.

	1	2	3	4	5	6
1 -----	2	3	4	5	6	7
2 -----	3	4	5	6	7	8
3 -----	4	5	6	7	8	9
4 -----	5	6	7	8	9	10
5 -----	6	7	8	9	10	11
6 -----	7	8	9	10	11	12

This is the only time when you are in a casino that you can make a true-odds bet, one in which you and the house are on equal footing. Well, sorta. Casinos did not become big and rich by being *that* fair. So to make your chances of winning a little crapier, the house makes you put down *another* bet that is *not* true-odds. Here's how it works: You make a bet and throw the dice. If you roll a 7 or an 11, you win. Roll 2,

3 or 12 and you lose. Any other number becomes the "point." Roll the dice again, and if you manage to throw either a 7 or the point, you win. If some other number comes up, continue throwing until you hit a 7 or the point, since the game won't finish until you do. That is about all there is to it. There are other kinds of bets you can make, but if you are interested, you already know all this, and if this kind of gambling doesn't get your blood flowing, I'm sure this is all you care to know.

7 Ball

The 7 ball in this billiards game has a white number 7 in a red circle and a black stripe. Stick it in the middle of a round rack surrounded by balls numbered 1 through 6 in clockwise order, thank you very much. Hit the cue ball at the group. Your opponent then has to tell you which side of the table he thinks he will eventually pocket the number #7 ball. Now hit the cue ball so that it hits the number 1 ball, either rolling it into a pocket or, failing that, making the cue ball or the numbered ball hit a cushion. You win if you hit the number 7 ball into a pocket on the side of the table you said you would.

Billiards is played with seven solid-colored balls and a white cue ball.

Pool's 7 ball is a solid dark red with a black 7 in a white circle.

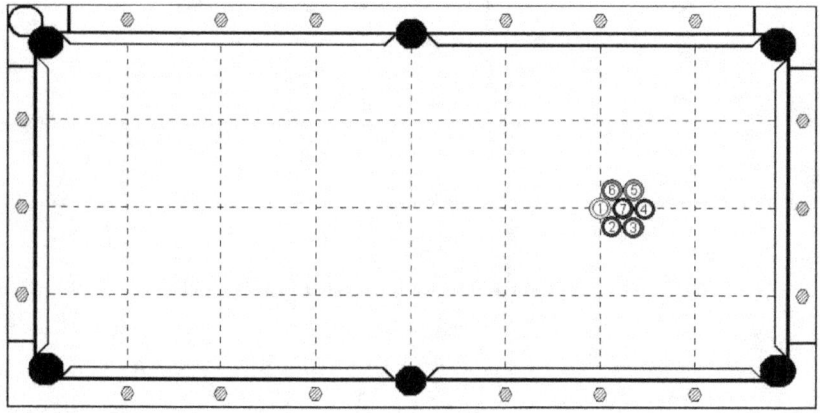

Seven-Card Stud

In this poker game, everybody antes. Each player is dealt two cards down and one up. They all bet. Then everyone is given another card face up. Bet again. Get two more face-up cards and bet after each one. Then you get the seventh card that only you can look at. Bet some more. Now everybody shows everybody else the five of their seven cards that make the best hand. Best hand wins everything in the pot. Take another drink of beer. Fart. Eat a couple of chips. Start over and continue until everyone is bored or broke.

Sevens (aka Parliament, Fan Tan, Card Dominoes)

The object here is to get rid of all your cards before anyone else does. On the first round, play a 7 if you have one, but pass if you don't. When someone else lays down a 7, you can play either up or down from it if you follow suit. They say in the rules that if you *can* play, you *can't* pass. I guess that's so you can't let someone else win, but I'm still studying on it.

Card Shuffling

It has been known for many, many years that in order to shuffle cards correctly—meaning that their new sort is as random as possible—you must shuffle the deck seven times. No more and no less. Persi Diaconis and Ron Graham have written *Magical Mathematics* and nicely explained this phenomenon. Quoting *The Wall Street Journal*'s review of the book:

> You have to shuffle seven times before a deck becomes truly scrambled. Not only that, the cards become mixed in a highly unusual way: The amount of randomness in the deck does not increase smoothly. The first few shuffles do little to disturb the original order, and even after six shuffles, you can still pick out distinctly non-random patches.
>
> But right around the seventh shuffle something remarkable happens. Shuffling hits its tipping point, and the cards rapidly decay into chaos.

The seven-shuffles finding applies to messy, imperfect riffle shuffles. The deck might not be divided exactly in half, for instance, or the cards might be riffled together in a haphazard way. Far from undesirable, a little sloppiness is actually the key to a random shuffle. [30]

Warning! You need to stop shuffling after the seventh time, because if you do happen to shuffle the deck exactly perfectly, the eighth shuffle will return the deck to its original configuration.

Mashie Niblick

Mashie Niblick is what we used to call a 7 iron golf club. Now I'm all about simplifying, but aren't there some things that were fine and dandy just the way they were? Many years ago golfers lamented that there was a void in their bags. Something was needed for those in-between shots—the ones too short for a mashie, a longish iron, and too long for a niblick, a wedge with good loft. So here came the mashie niblick to solve the problem. Pretty simple. But golfers of the last century changed the romantic names of the irons to numbers. So now the mashie niblick is just a 7.

"Mashie niblick" was listed in a dictionary of difficult words, printed in the United Kingdom just a couple years ago. Perhaps in deference to our verbally challenged neighbors, we should continue saying "7 iron" until such time as that also becomes too difficult.

Seven Wood

Golfers also use woods in addition to irons, and the smallest one in use is the 7. It's great for some shots, but I haven't discovered yet which ones. Nor have I seen anyone else use a 7 wood since the first tournament I was in. I was twenty-one and proudly shooting my weight. My partner was on the back side of eighty years old, shooting her age, and played the entire round with this club.

The Seven Blocks of Granite

Waaaaay back in 1936 the Fordham University football team was facing what might have been their best season and a trip to the Rose Bowl. Timothy Cohane, the school publicist, thought a nickname was just the ticket to get some ink for their offensive line. (He had thought this for several seasons, trying first to get "Seven Samsons" to catch on.) Then, borrowing from another reporter, he named the center, two guards, two ends, and two linemen the Seven Blocks of Granite—and folks loved it. The players were: Al Babartsky, Johnny Druze, Ed Franco, Leo Paquin, Natty Pierce, Alex Wojciechowicz and Vince Lombardi. They never made it to the Rose Bowl.

The Stanley Cup and the Silver Seven

Hockey fans all know the Stanley Cup is the championship best-of-seven series of games to determine the world's best professional team. Prior to 1910, any team could participate, even if they were amateur. So in 1903, '04, and '05, the Ottawa Silver Seven won. That was reported by the *New York Public Library Desk Reference*. However, it was really the Ottawa Senators. The team had several nicknames—most famously, the Silver Seven of early hockey legend—but was generally known throughout its history as the Senators.

Tangram

Start with a square. Divide it into seven parts that include five triangles, a square, and a rhomboid. Now take these seven pieces and create other pictures with them. According to tradition—dating back to China 4,000 years ago—that is exactly what happened when a man dropped a tile. When it shattered into seven pieces, he tried to reconstruct the square. When they didn't fit together again as a square, he noticed his incorrect assemblages made some interesting patterns. Thus was born *ch'i ch'iao tu*, or the Seven-Piece Wisdom Board.

Chapter 4

NATURE AND GEOGRAPHY

Nature delights in the number seven.
-Philo Judaeus, Alexandrian philosopher

T HIS CHAPTER IS about reality – those seven-things we find
in the natural and the physical world. When most plants and
animals have either one or two of something, we have found
many instances where seven occurs in their structure. Let's talk about
the places that are known for being one of seven – the wonders of the
world, the seas, the continents. We'll look at all the places with seven
in their names and find out how that came to be.

PEOPLE

Seven Smells

T HE THEORY THAT humans have seven basic smells has been
tossed about for the last 2,000 years, but we're still trying
to figure it all out. The theory says that our olfactory bulbs,

actually part of our brains, have seven different-shaped receptors. An odor is essentially a teeny tiny bit *of* a thing which breaks off, becomes airborne, and wafts into our nose. I think I can actually live with that knowledge unless someone tells me these tiny particles are at least large enough to carry germs with them . . . ewww. At any rate, these smells are shaped differently and must fit into the receptors. You won't easily find the names of the seven described the same way by two scientists, but here is the list I use: alcohol, peppermint, flowers, musk, camphor (like moth balls), vinegar, and sulfur (rotten eggs).

Endocrines

The endocrine system is the corporate headquarters for all the major functions carried out by the body. The seven major glands (the regional offices) are adrenal cortex, endocrine pancreas, medulla, ovaries (or testes in men), parathyroids, pituitary, and thyroid. Each one sends out their designated workers, in the form of hormones, throughout the body to control what all the parts are supposed to be doing, to coordinate the schedules, and to communicate messages while away on the business trips. They are responsible to oversee growth (mergers and acquisitions), or downsizing, metabolism (Do we need a layoff or overtime? Is this body working hard or hardly working?) and homeostasis (are we all working on the same corporate agenda?)

Blood and Skin

An average woman has about seven pints of blood in her body. (A man of the same weight has more.) Since a pint weighs a pound, she will have seven pounds of blood. A stone equals about seven pounds, so an English woman will have a stone of blood. (There used to be a clever joke there, but something got lost in that translation.)

Your heart pumps blood at about .7 miles per hour.

Skin is the largest organ in the human body; an average person has seven pounds of skin. You'll even hear it argued that there are seven layers of skin.

Seventh Nerve

Gray's Anatomy describes the seventh nerve, or cranial nerve, as the one that controls facial expressions. So it's the one that lets you raise your eyebrows and make that "wow!" expression you get when reading all the amazing stuff in this book. It also controls tearing, salivation, and important parts of your sense of taste and hearing. Without control of this nerve structure you would look slack-jawed, drooling, unblinking, staring. Most unfortunately, this sometimes happens to young ladies (often during pregnancy) as well as newborn babies (due to birth trauma.) They call this seventh-nerve palsy, or Bell's palsy. Who else is at risk? Anyone with diabetes, the flu, or even a common cold. How scary it *that*? On the bright side, many people see signs of improvement after only a couple of weeks and most within a few months.

The Seven Senses

The ancients believed there are seven senses, and after seeing the list—touch, taste, smell, sight, hearing, speech, and animation—it still doesn't make much sense to me. Animation in this context represents willed movement, and speech is a function of animation plus thought. Don't you think *thought* should be on the list? I do rather like Marilyn vos Savant's take on the matter, though. She says, "Senses are arbitrary labels. And if we're ever better able to examine any sort of extrasensory perception . . . . . . we will have taken a step in the direction of creating one. At that point, we would probably demystify it by giving it a name . . . Aspiring [a] seventh . . . would be handled in the same way." [31]

People centuries ago had things pretty well thought out when it came to body functions. Quoting from the *Brewer's Dictionary of Phrases and Fable*:

> *According to the very ancient teaching, the soul of man, or his "inward holy body," is compounded of the seven properties which are under the influence of the seven planets. Fire animates, earth gives the sense of feeling, water gives speech, air*

gives taste, mist gives sight, flowers give hearing, and the south wind gives smelling. Hence the seven senses are animation, feeling, speech, taste, sight, hearing and smelling. [32]

So the "seven senses," rather than relating to our physical abilities, relates to our spiritual nature.

Ear Growth

Jos Verhulst and Patrick Onghena took a very long time doing research on men's ear growth rates. Because that is so fundamental to our self-knowledge. And will save the world from blight. And pestilence. But no matter—what they found was that man's ear-growth-rate peaks every seven years. *Science Frontiers*, No. 111: May-Jun 1997, published their finding and titled the article "Circaseptennial Rhythm in Ear Growth."

And like it or not, Verhulst and Onghena weren't the first guys with so little on their agendas that they studied this phenomenon. An anonymous writer in *Science News*, 151:26 1997 wrote an article, which cited British Medical Journal, 12/21/96, and so on back to the ancient Greeks, those sages who coined the term *circaseptennial* in the first place.

Septuplets

Seven sets of septuplets have reportedly been born, the first set in 1985. (Although one source claims to have identified fifty-five.) Unsurprisingly, not all seven of any single birth usually survive. Today, there are three surviving sets: The McCaughey's, born November 19, 1997 in Des Moines, Iowa are the first to live past infancy; the Humair children were born January 14, 1998 in Abha, Saudi Arabia; and the Khamis family's, born August 16, 2008 in Alexandria, Egypt.

Shorties:

* Your head has seven holes in it: two eyes, two ears, two nostrils, and a mouth.

* You have seven tarsal bones in each foot.

✳ You have only seven pairs of true ribs, that is, ones that are attached to the sternum.

✳ The largest organ in the human body is the skin. Taken from an "average" person, it weighs seven pounds.

✳ There are now seven billion humans on earth.

ANIMALS

Seven-Level Classification

Carl Linnaeus (1707-1778) was a persistent fellow—determined to name every plant and animal, and do so in a consistent and logical way. Although it has been modified many times, he chose a **seven-level classification system**: kingdom, phylum, class, order, family, genus, and species. He defined these seven classifications from the broadest (kingdom is either animal or vegetable) to progressively more specific characterizations until you get to the very last two, which are used for the scientific name of the thing. The scientific world still uses this system today.

Seven Life Processes

Although they eventually morph into each other, animals and vegetables have functions of life that separate them from the minerals. The animal kingdom is separated from the vegetable's because they have a couple of extra talents—although some folks will disagree and talk to their plants as if they can be heard and will argue further that there are some plants that can move. But I didn't come here to argue.

There are seven systems that set animals apart from rocks, two of which also are characteristics we have that plants do not:

✳ Respiration

✳ Growth

✳ Nutrition

* Excretion

* Reproduction

* Sensitivity

* Movement

Spiders

Almost all ordinary spiders produce seven different kinds of silk for their webs—five for spinning the web itself (with varying combinations of strength, stickiness, and elasticity,) another with which to wrap its victims, and the seventh to wrap its eggs. It takes seven different genes, not surprisingly, each with its own gland, to generate this variety.

Spider legs, all eight of them, have seven joints. Want them named? Coxa, trochanter, femur, patella, tibia, metatarsus, and tarsus.

Roly-poly Bugs

Do you see pill bugs around your house? You know, those cute little buggers that look like miniature armadillos and roll into a ball when you pick them up? (In some parts of the country, they are called sow bugs or woodlice.) Take a closer look and – you'll see they have seven pairs of legs. Truthfully, they aren't really bugs at all; bugs are certain kinds of insects and insects have only three pairs of legs. These guys are really crustaceans—like lobsters and crabs—and they actually breathe through gills, even though they live on dry land. They usually are fairly beneficial, but could maybe start nibbling on your young garden plants. So the advice then is to trap them with a piece of cantaloupe. Personally, I'd rather eat the cantaloupe myself and let these little guys eat what they want. I think they're cool.

Scorpions

Scorpions are closely related to spiders, but instead of biting, the business end is on the infamous tail you see curled up over their backs. This stinger is called the cephalothorax and it is divided into seven segments. The last one is the one to avoid.

Figure-Seven Moth

On a much more appealing note, the figure-seven moth (*Synedoida grandirena*) is much less likely to give you a start, but you are much less likely to ever see one at all, as they are rather rare, emerging into adulthood in the late spring or early summer and only in the Midwestern United States. The figure seven appears on the wings when the moth is at rest.

Burgess Shale

Another animal you won't likely see—having been extinct for rather more than a few years—is the Burgess Shale, discovered by C. D. Walcott in 1909 and named *Hallucigenia* by Simon Conway Morris. It had seven pairs of tentacles, which may or may not have been used as legs and also seven pairs of spines, which may or may not have been used in defense or offense.

Seven-Spot Archer Fish

The seven-spot archer fish (*Toxotes charareus*) is a native of Asia and Oceania. It is a predator that can grow up to nearly twelve inches (30cm), so it is not a great choice to put into your tank. They live in brackish waters, anyway, and all your friends will keep telling you that the water needs to be cleaned and filtered. Not surprisingly, the fish have seven dark blotches along their bodies.

Broadnose Sevengill Shark

The Broadnose sevengill shark is a species that lives in the South Pacific, South Atlantic, and Indian Oceans. You'll know it when you see it, because besides having a broad nose, it has seven pairs of gill slits, and most sharks have only five. It also has only a single dorsal fin. But saying Broadnose Sevengill Singledorsalfin Shark is hard. Especially when you see one and are trying to warn your diving partner. The scientific name is *Notorynchus cepedianus*, which isn't any easier to say. But never fear—there have been no confirmed attacks on people, and there just aren't that many of these sharks around anyway.

Seven-Arm Octopus

If you do any deep sea diving, see if you can spot a seven-arm octopus (*Haliphron atlanticus*). They are very big, but very rare. If you find one with only seven arms, it's a male. Actually, this isn't true. Oh, it's a male alright, and you'll only see seven arms, but in fact there is an eighth. It is called a *hectocotylus*, which is a special appendage used for fertilizing eggs, and is kept discretely tucked away in a sac beneath its eye. I'll give you folks a moment to picture that in your mind.

Horseshoe Crabs

There have been more than one fossil species of horseshoe crabs found that have seven sets of legs. (The ones you see today only have 6 pairs.) But I'm thinking that if enough of you people start checking, we're going to find a species with seven still around. You read about things like that happening. If you're the one making this discovery, you'll probably get the beast named after you, which would be a lot of fun.

Queen Snake

Often mistaken for a garter snake, this gal is gray with two "peach or light yellow stripe[s] down its body . . . and two ventral stripes . . . toward the neck." (Sounds lovely, doesn't it? Not too many animals of *any* kind are gray and peach.) There are three other stripes along its back, making seven stripes in all and accounting for the scientific name *Regina septemvittata*, which literally translates "queen of seven stripes." These snakes are very picky about where they live, since their diet is mostly crawdads. They are only active from May to *Sept*ember, and then hibernate the other *seven* months of the year. And here's irony: during hibernation, crawdads feed on *them*!

Dog Years

We've all heard this one: Multiply your dog's age by seven and you will find its equivalent in human years. (People say this about cats, too.) Is it true? Well not really—it's way too general. Think about it: *many* dogs live to be 16 years old, but how many people are alive at 112? And if the dog is a year and a half old and mature enough to reproduce, would a child be at ten and a half? The middle years of cats and dogs—say, from four to ten—do in fact fairly well correspond to this formula. So if you want to keep on saying "seven dog years equal one human year," be my guest.

Pixie-Bob Cat

The pixie-bob cat is an odd breed of house cat. Tradition says it is a mix of a feral bobcat and a domestic, but that's just one of those things that people say because they heard it. The interesting thing about this cat is that it is polydactyl – it has seven toes. In fact, the pixie-bob is the only breed of cat accepted by any of the big cat-lover/breeder/show-cat associations that *is* polydactyl. Not that *other* breeds of cats are polydactyl, except for aberrations of nature. All other cats have five toes on the front paws and four on the back paws.

Dinosaurs

So far, scientists have identified and named only seven dinosaurs after the places where their fossils were found:

* Albertosaurus—from Alberta, Canada

* Andesurus—located in the Andes Mountains of South America

* Coloradisaurus—found in Colorado

* Denversaurus—dug up in Denver, Colorado

* Indosarus—found in India

* Lesothosaurus—from Lesotho, South Africa

* Szechuanosarus—discovered in the Szechuan area of China

Eggs and Chickens

The record for a hen laying eggs: seven in one day.

Chickens have seven different kinds of combs: rose, strawberry, single, cushion, buttercup, pea, and V. I'll bet none of your friends know that. I'll bet even Ken Jennings doesn't know that.

Vertebrae

A giraffe has only seven vertebrae bones in his neck. And so do you. And so does an elephant and a rat and a cat and a bat. So perhaps this isn't big news. What may be more interesting is that there seem to be only two mammals that do *not*: the two-toed sloth and a manatee. There have been several publications that explain why this may be so, and they all involve the lack of speed the manatee and sloth exhibit, which is why they have evolved with only six vertebrae and it is a natural defense against cancer because of the *Hox* gene expression and oxidative damage to DNA and such things.

PLANTS

Seven-Year Apple (*Genipa clusiifolia* or *Casasia clusiifolia*)

The first variety, which used to grow only in the West Indies, has been transplanted very successfully in Florida, and is often used as a windbreaker along highways. *Casasia clusiifolia*, pronounced "kuh-saw-see-uh kloo-see-if-fole-ee-uh", is its cousin and is a native to Florida. Both grow heartily in the salty air and little fresh water, so are well-suited to your beachfront property. Their fleshy black fruit is edible, but you don't often see it in the local markets, do you?

Seven-Angle Pipewort (*Eriocaulon aquaticum*), a.k.a. hatpins

These plants are seriously a lot more fun than it sounds. Don't they really, really look just like hat pins? (Does anyone really *really* remember what a hat pin looks like?) Anyway, these are flowers that grow in ponds in the northeastern part of the United States and up into Canada a bit. They poke their little reedy, leafless selves out of the water about six inches or so and out pops a small dirty-white puff of a flower. But on to its seven: its stalk has seven sides! Woo hoo!

Seven Top Turnip (*Brassica septiceps*)

Said to be delicious with tender green leaves, this vegetable can be harvested all winter. On sale now from the Burpee catalogue.

Seven Son Flower (*heptacodium miconioides*)

This is a great deciduous shrub growing to about fifteen inches high and wide. It produces small white flowers in clusters of seven, which turn red as they develop in late summer and last until the first frost.

Gentiana Septemfida Lagodechiana

This cornflower-blue ten-inch perennial plant, blooming in July and August, has bell-shaped blossoms in clusters of seven. Native to the Alpine, it thrives in high elevations and is often used in rock gardens. The *septemfida* means "having seven divisions."

Kalopanax Septemlobus

This is a deciduous tree that grows in China and Japan. It has seven-lobed leaves, small yellow-green flowers, and blue-black berries. You can make a tasty tea from the leaves, but as the same concoction is also used as an insecticide, do you really want to?

Indian Rhododendron (*Melastoma septemnervium*)

Little is found about this plant, other than it has seven-veined leaves and is considered a weed.

Seven Barks

Have you taken a close look at your Hydrangea arborescens lately? Its common name is seven barks, for reasons that are obvious when you discover the multi-colored layers of bark on the bushes. The native Indians used the plant to dissolve kidney and bladder stones and as a diuretic and tonic. But beware: excessive use will leave you light-headed. The bark was also used as a poultice on open wounds and burns and was chewed to relieve tummy aches.

Starflower (*Trientalis borealis*)

Growing only in the mid- to northeastern United States and northeastern Canada, this is one of the rare seven-petaled flowers to exist anywhere on earth. This perennial rhizome is only about six inches tall and has white, star-shaped flowers three to a stalk. It has seven sepals, slender and pointy, seven petals, slender and pointy, and seven stamens of vivid yellow that are not slender and pointy.

The Maneau Ra (*Konori x christianae*)

This is a tall dramatic plant with seven peach-colored petals that turn a bright coral as they mature.

Other Seven Plants

There are many plants and flowers with *seven* in their commercial names that do not have seven anything about them physically. Here are a few:

* ✳ Rose—Seven Sisters (*Rosa multiflora*)

* ✳ Hosta—Seventh Heaven

* ✳ Daylilies—Double Oh Seven, Twin Seven Seven, Seventh Day, Seven Spanish Angels, Seven Devils, Seven Days Battles, Lucky Seven, Iona Seventh Day

* ✳ Iris—Double Oh Seven

* ✳ Hibiscus—Goulding Seven (*Hibiscus rosa-sinensis*), R A N &

Seven (*Hibiscus rosa-sinensis*), Seven Sisters (*Hibiscus rosa-sinensis*), Seven Veils (*Hibiscus rosa-sinensis*)

✳ Hydrangea—Wild Sevenbark 'Annabell' (*Hydrangea arborenscens*)

✳ Tomato—Ohio WR Seven (*Lycopersicon lycopersicum*)

✳ Candlebush—Seven Golden Candlesticks (*Cassia alata*)

The Seven Fruits of Israel

Deuteronomy 8:8 describes what has come to be known as the seven grains (or fruits) of Israel: "a land of wheat and barley and vines and fig trees and pomegranates; a land of olive oil and honey." Those Hebrews—thinking honey is a plant. Tsk, tsk. The seven are usually now defined as dates, olives, figs, grapes, pomegranates, wheat, and barley.

Old World Medicines

Did you ever wonder what on earth those magical ingredients are in the old books about the plants that shamans and "doctors" and witches used to brew? Sadly, perhaps, "eye of newt" wasn't really the orbs of lizards, nor were many other odd things what they sound like. In order to disguise what they were really using, pseudonames were given to otherwise common plants.

Here are some examples: Parsley was called devil's oatmeal, and was used to rid oneself of the ghosts hovering around. It also allowed you to talk to the dead. The seven-connection comes from the saying that the reason it takes parsley so long to sprout is because it must first go to Hel and back seven times. (And no, Hel is not misspelled—they aren't talking about going to hell, but to Hel, the ancient goddess.)

Yarrow was renamed Seven Year's Love and was used in love potions. Hel also loved Seven Year's Love, and would come to your aid if you offered it to her while in the midst of a battle.

OUR WORLD

The Seven Seas

Let's assume that the world's waters are somehow divided, because men throughout the ages have decided there are seven oceans. (We are still researching to find the dividing lines and so the exact parameters will be available soon.) For the record, today, these seven seas are defined as the Arctic, Antarctic, North Pacific, South Pacific, North Atlantic, South Atlantic and the Indian. I say "today", because men have made references to the Seven Seas long before they could have been aware of a couple of them, so the old seven were a different seven.

And, the term Seven Seas has also been a designation for the "principal seas of navigation and trade." When *that* is what was meant, they were talking about the Arabian Sea, the Atlantic Ocean, the Bay of Bengal, the Mediterranean Sea, the Persian Gulf, the Red Sea and the South China Sea.

Seven Continents

What would better complement the seven bodies of water than seven bodies of land? Hence, we also have seven continents, which says more about our political leanings than our geographic skills. They are: Europe, Asia, Africa, North America, South America, Antarctica, and Australia.

Seven Natural Wonders of the World

Being still too young for a consensus to be established, which would make one list the one *true* list, here is the truly unscientifically researched established list of the Seven Natural Wonders of the World:

The Grand Canyon, Arizona, US—If measured from Glen Canyon Dam at one end to Lake Mead at the other, the canyon is about 275 miles long. Five miles wide at the narrowest point and eighteen at the widest, it is almost exactly one mile deep. Evidence finds that there has been human habitation at the Grand Canyon for more than

4,000 years, the earliest known people being Paleo-Indian, then the members of the desert culture of which little is known. Following were the Anasazi, or "The Ancient Ones," who occupied the premises from around 700 to 1100 CE before disappearing for unknown reasons. Europeans arrived in 1540 when Captain Garcia Lopez de Cardenas, having been sent by Coronado to find the Seven Cities of Gold, spent three days there. It would be three centuries before Captain John Wesley Powell and troops would return. In 1882 then-Senator Benjamin Harrison first introduced legislation to create Grand Canyon National Park, but it was not until 1918 that the bill finally passed.

It should also be noted that the erosion of the canyon walls let us see that the area has been under seas on seven different occasions in its geographic life.

The Great Barrier Reef, Queensland, Australia—Not only is the Great Barrier Reef one of the Natural Wonders of the World, it is the largest *animal-made* structure on earth. At 345,000 square kilometers, it is also the world's largest protected marine area. Actually, it is a 1,250-mile-long chain of coral reefs made of the skeletons of billions and billions of tiny polyps all cemented together with algae-produced limestone. The varying colors and shapes of the coral are a result of the many hundreds and hundreds of different kinds of polyps represented in the formation. It is amazing and amazing.

The Harbor of Rio de Janeiro—"Discovered" by Portuguese explorers on January 1, 1502, this wonderful harbor of course had been known to the native Tupi Indians as Guanabara, which translates to "arm of the sea." The deep waters can accommodate the largest ships, but time and people have shrunk the footprint. Surrounded by low but impressive mountains which hug the harbor beaches, the waters have not been improved upon by the pollutants poured into it. But, hey, you're there. It's Mardi Gras. It's Carnival. Your Japanese friend speaks perfect Portuguese and the music's intoxicating. Who cares?

Mount Everest—Located in Nepal and known as Chomolungma to the local Tibetans, this mammoth mountain does not stand alone.

It is amid the Himalayas, a range of mammoths. Let's agree that the height of 29,028 feet is high, and "because it's there" it lures adventurers and thrill-seekers in amazing numbers. Edmund Hillary and the Sherpa Tenzing Norgay (why don't we ever remember *his* name?) led the hordes by becoming the first men to reach the summit only 50 years ago.

Victoria Falls—The locals of Zimbabwe know this place as Mosi-oa-Tunya, "the smoke that thunders" and they aren't kidding! The roar of the water can be heard from twenty-five miles away. And the mist produced can be seen from about the same distance. We are told. The Zambezi River provides the water that spreads out almost a mile wide before it drops the 420 feet. David Livingstone (we presume) gets the credit for "discovering" the falls in 1855 and graciously named them after his queen.

Paricutin Volcano—Until early 1943, the west central Mexican town of San Juan Parangaricutiro was a quiet little corn-farming community. The next day, and almost every day for the next nine years, a volcano spewed millions and millions of tons of lava, transforming the valley into a remarkable pile two thousand feet high.

Aurora Borealis—Latin for "northern dawn" but often referred to as the Northern Lights, it is one phenomenal display of luminosity. Appearing in a variety of forms and shapes, it can be viewed as streamers, rays, draperies, arcs, and banks of colors that move and weave and wax and wane. Red, yellow, green, blue, violet—the colors meld and flow as a probable result of electrons and protons from the sun being attracted to the earth's polar fields and excited into visibility. Or something. We don't care, do we? Although most readily seen in the northern reaches of the world, and most often and most vividly during equinoxes, sunspot activity and magnetic storms, I have personally seen them as far south as Denver, Colorado.

And then of course, there is a similar (actually identical) phenomenon in the southern hemisphere—the Aurora Australis. Catch the show. It'll knock your socks off.

NORTH AMERICAN "SEVEN" CITIES

SEVEN HILLS, ALABAMA—THERE are about ten miles between Mobile, Alabama, and the border of Mississippi. At about the midway point you'll go through Seven Hills. Do not blink or you'll already be past it. Population about 3,830; ZIP 36608.

Seven Springs, Arizona—Hey, when you get to Phoenix you're almost there, so take another fifteen minutes and drive north on I-17 to the—well, no, you better take the Carefree Highway as if you were headed to the Horseshoe Dam. But don't turn east and if you get to Cordes Junction or a paved road, you've gone too far. But since there's only one way there you can't miss it. ZIP 85377.

Seven Oaks, California—Population 650. ZIP 92305. As the crow flies, this isn't far from San Bernadino, but you can't get there from there. Just completed in November of 1999, the US Army Corps of Engineers built the Seven Oaks Dam. "Seven Oaks Dam has removed the most massive flooding problem west of the Mississippi River, eliminating a floodplain previously threatening more than three million people . . . recently presented with an Honor Award by the Chief of Engineers Design and Environmental Awards Program." [32] Oh my!

Seven Trees, California—Population "856 males and 810 females." ZIP 95111. Situated just a couple of miles southeast of San Jose, this is a youngish town of largely Hispanic and other other-than-white folks, 56 percent of whom are thirty-ish and single. That's about 480 unmarried men, (take note all you single-and-looking gals), and their unemployment rate is below the state average and the price of the houses is above the median for California. (So, all you men of Seven Trees, if you soon notice a large influx of available women around town, you have me to thank. And you are more than welcome. I try to help whenever I can.)

Seven Hickories, Delaware—Northwest of Dover, only about fifteen miles from the Delaware River and half that distance from Route 1, it is what we have come to know and love as a wide spot in the road. There's a rumor that the "Welcome to Seven Hickories" sign says "Welcome to Seven Hickories" on both sides. ZIP 19904.

Seven Rivers, New Mexico—Just off Highway 285 north of the Carlsbad Caverns lies Seven Rivers. Named for the North Seven Rivers (there is only *one* river; no South Seven Rivers exists), the claim to fame here was the gang known as the Seven Rivers Warriors. This group of usually law-abiding citizens took to rustling cattle from John Chisum (of the Chisum trail fame), whose large herds were hoarding all the hay. The seven in the name came from the seven arroyos that fed into the Pecos River thereabouts. Listed some places as merely a ghost town, it's still on the maps. ZIP 88254. The population in 2000 was 225. Today the population is zero. But the ZIP code is still there.

Seven Springs, North Carolina—In the eastern part of the state just off I-70, this village of only eighty-six people is a great farming region and has a good supply of water from the springs. We assume. We can't understand why so many would leave; the population has dwindled by half in the last decade. ZIP code 28578. Population is 4,209.

Seven Lakes, North Carolina—ZIP code 27376. Population 3,214. This is one of our newer towns, (really a "master planned community") developed in the early 1970s as a weekend or vacation spot, but the year-round ownership is growing. And no, there are not seven lakes.

Seven Devils, North Carolina—Amy Keller, the town clerk, tells me that this new town—it was only incorporated in 1979—has 129 permanent residents. Their new ZIP code is 28604. Ms. Keller relates that the founding fathers, seven men, observed the seven surrounding mountains, knew a local with seven sons "as mean as devils," learned that winters were cold as the devil, and—hey, they wanted a catchy name, so Seven Devils it is. They have more going for them than many places ten times their size: golf course, ski slope, a lake, campground, stables, police and fire Departments, zoning, and sits in the Blue Ridge Mountains . Sounds like seventh heaven to me.

Seven Hills, Ohio—This is another one of our newest (incorporated in 1961) and largest (population 20,947) of the "seven" cities. Located in northern Ohio, it is a suburb of Cleveland. ZIP 44131.

Seven Mile, Ohio—Sitting on the banks of **Seven Mile Creek** is this burg of 678 souls. It's just north of Cincinnati, so why not stop in sometime? How often have you visited a burg of souls? ZIP 45062.

Seven Pines, Pennsylvania—Not being listed on many maps, do you think any of the 1,609 residents are offended? Or do they like that? Shall we all write post cards and ask? ZIP 17082.

Seven Stars, Pennsylvania—"From antiquity, people have been fond of using the number seven in naming their properties." That's their explanation for the town's name, and this is a great little place between Altoona and State College; population 2,920; ZIP 17062.

Seven Springs, Pennsylvania—Not much here but the 127 people and a ski resort. But, hey, what else do you need? It's only about an hour's drive from Pittsburgh and a couple hundred miles from D.C. They still do not have their own ZIP code. The town is almost exactly a mile square and a square mile. And they can explain the difference.

Seven Valleys, Pennsylvania—South of York, this farming area boasts 2,681 residents. ZIP 17360.

Seven Sisters, Texas—Just forty miles west of Corpus Christi, rumor has it that the town was named for an oil field. Now let's find out why the oil field was named Seven Sisters: "The name of the community was translated from Spanish Siete Hermanas and refers either to seven small mounds in the area or, more likely, to the seven daughters of an important local landowner, Refugio Serna." ZIP 78357; population 533.

Seven Points, Texas—Located southeast of Dallas by the Cedar Creek Reservoir, this place has grown from about 720 residents in 1990 to 1,145 at last count. The economy thrives on oil, gas, and agriculture. ZIP 75143.

Seven Oaks, Texas—We are feverishly hoping that each one of the 131 folks who live here will buy this book, as I have promised to list their names in the revised second edition. The Handbook of Texas Online says the name was taken in honor of the English estate of the founder. ZIP 77350.

Seven Rivers, Texas—We can't find this place on a map and we can't find it with the census folks, but we did find a post office, so it must be there somewhere. ZIP 88254.

Seven Pines, Texas—Our government says that 14,025 folks live here, but doesn't tell where here is. We finally found it just north of Farm to Market road. ZIP 75644. And let's not confuse this place with:

Seven Pines, Virginia—Historically noted because of the Seven Pines Battle in the Civil War (see the chapter 6, "History and Government"), this town has the Seven Pines National Cemetery and the Richmond Airport.

Seven Mile Ford, Virginia—With 124 residents, if you are here, you are just north of the Tennessee-North Carolina border.

Seven Fountains, Virginia—Population 1,003, this little town is in the George Washington National Forest in the northern part of the state. ZIP 22652.

Seven Corners, Virginia—Just across the Potomac River from Washington D.C., Seven Corners has a population of 13,780; ZIP 22044. What seven streets converge to make the seven corners? Wilson Blvd., E. Broad St., Hillwood Ave., Arlington Blvd., Sleepy Hollow Rd., and Leesburg Pike. Yes, I *understand* this is only six, but find me a map that shows a seventh and I'll be grateful. Maybe Arlington Blvd. counts twice, since it inters the intersection at one angle and exits at another. . .

Seven Mile, Washington— This is a small town just north of Spokane and is on the border of Riverside State Park. ZIP 99208.

Seven Bays, Washington—Located by Lake Roosevelt in Roosevelt National Park, this small town is in the Big Bend region of eastern Washington, known for its good fishing and big wheat fields. They don't have their own ZIP code, and really isn't a town, but only a "populated place."

IT MUST BE that in the United States, the people decide to call places "seven-blah-blah" much more frequently than our government has seen fit to *officially* name these spots. We have found, oh, just about a thousand place names recorded by the US Bureau of Census. Are you ready for a list of some of them? The ones designated as either "unincorporated," a "minor civil subdivision that is not coextensive with an incorporated place," a "nonfunctioning or disorganized township," or an "inactive or nonfunctioning minor civil division."? Hey, while I'm at it, I'm going to throw in some place names that local folks use too.

Alabama – Seven Pines, Seven Hundred Thirty Mile Spur, Seven Hills
Arizona – Sevenmile

California – Seven Pines

Colorado – Seven Lakes, Sevenmile Plaza

Delaware – Seven Hickories

Florida – Seven Springs

Georgia – Bry-Man Seven Cities Plaza

Illinois – Township of Seven Hickory, Seven Hills

Indiana – Seven Springs

Kentucky – Seven Corners

Maine – Township of Seven Ponds

Maryland – Seven Oaks

Michigan – Seven Harbors, Seven Oaks, White Lake-Seven Harbors

Mississippi – Seven Pines, Seven Springs

Missouri – Seven Pines

Montana – Number Seven

Nevada – Seven Troughs and a Tunnel

New Jersey – Seven Stars (in two counties: Ocean County and Salem County)

New Mexico – Seven Lakes, Seven Rivers, Seven Springs

North Carolina – Seven Bridges, Seven Creeks, Seven Devils (again, it is in two counties - Avery County and Watauga County,) Seven Lakes, Seven Springs, Seven Paths

Ohio – Seven Hills (in Hamilton County and Cuyahoga County)

Oklahoma – Seven Oaks

Oregon – Seven Oaks

Pennsylvania – Seven Pines, Seven Points, Seven Stars (*Five* of them! – Adams, Huntingdon, Chester, Montgomery, and Juniata counties) Seven Springs (another two-fer – Somerset and Fayette counties) Seven Fields

South Carolina – Sevenmile (just a note here – very often, in fact almost all of the time, Sevenmile is run together as a single word. Don't ask us why. Maybe those folks are agoraphobic and don't like open spaces. This is done for other place-names, too, like Sevenoaks.) Seven Oaks (already with the exceptions to the exceptions)

South Dakota –Seven Mile Corner (a little community of people living at the entrance to the Badlands National Monument, seven miles from Kadoka, if you need a point of reference to a well-known city.)

Tennessee – Seven Cedars, Seven Islands, Sevenoaks

Texas – Seven Points (in Henderson and Kaufman Counties.)

Utah – Seven Mile

Virginia – Seven Islands, Septa

Washington – Seven Mile

Wisconsin – Town of Seven Mile Creek

Virgin Islands – Seven Hills

The pick of the day? The honor, according to us, goes to Seven Troughs and a Tunnel, Nevada. Located in Pershing County, it was once the home to almost 250 ditch-diggers. Established in 1907 at the onset of the mining frenzy of Nevada, STaaT reached its hiatus and demise within eleven years and all that now remains is a few building foundations and rutty roads. However, with an elevation of 7,474 feet, the nearby Seven Troughs Mountain is not likely to disappear anytime soon. Perhaps it should also be noted that Nevada has a couple other "Seven" Mountains: Seven Lakes Mountain, 6,049 feet, in Washoe County, and Sevenmile Point in White Pine County, which towers 6,470 feet.

Seven Sacred Pools

Located within the Haleakala National Park on the Hawaiian island of Maui, this area is really named Ohe'o Gulch. The Pipiwai stream runs from the nearby mountain and into the Pacific, carving the series of many-more-than seven basins along the way. In a stroke of advertising genius, a hotel created the name in an effort to entice more visitors to the area. It worked, and no one ever seems bothered when they find nothing sacred. Or seven.

Seven Caves, Bainbridge, Ohio

Open all year 'round, this area is an Ohio National Landmark. It boasts natural anomalies like plants and animals that should not, by all rights, be there. There is plenty of hiking and outdoor recreation, fishing, birding, and of course, spelunking. And the caves are reportedly haunted.

Sevens in South Dakota

Seven Pine Hill (in Meade County), Seven Springs (in Bon Homme County (there *used* to be seven springs, but now there are more), Seven Mile Creek (in Charles Mix County; yep, looks like this tributary of the Missouri River is seven miles long.)

Sevens in Kansas

Sevenmile Creek (yes, it *is* seven miles long), Seven Springs (there are actually two such locations in the state – one on the boarder of Sumner and Cowley counties and the other over in Scott County. The former was known as Geuda by the local Ponca Indians and was visited by them because the mineral-rich waters had healing powers. Rumor has it that at one time developers had hopes that this area would become as popular as Hot Springs, Arkansas and Saratoga Springs of New York.)

Sevenmile Hill, Nebraska

Sevenmile Hill. Have any of you been to Nebraska? Remember the roller coaster ride of driving up and down all those hills? Well neither do I, to tell the truth. But there are hills there. They are just hidden a little behind the corn cribs. Sevenmile Hill towers a dizzying 1,130 feet above that fruited plain in the north central part of the state.

Seven Devils, Idaho and Oregon

This is a mountain range located beside Hells Canyon, the deepest gorge in the United States, at the bottom of which is the Snake River. Take US Federal Highway 95 (not to be confused with US *Interstate* Highway mentioned below) to skirt the range. The Salmon River is on the other side of the mountains. He Devil is the highest of the mountains at 9,393 feet. But don't miss She Devil, Devils Throne, Tower of Babel, Twin Imps, The Ogre, or the Goblin. (This sounds like a theme park, doesn't it?) Local lore says it was the natives that named the range Seven Devils, and the Europeans named the individual peaks with suitable titles. You may want to do a drive-by to the Gospel Hump Wilderness just northeast, the Frank Church Wilderness of No Return to the east, and take a look at Heaven's Gate Lookout.

Seven Devils State Recreation Site, Oregon

Now pay attention: Although the Seven Devils Mountain range is in the northeast corner of Oregon, this *park* is ten miles north of Bandon, Oregon, which is near Coos Bay on the southwestern shore of the state. If you are traveling north on the 101 and get to Devils Lake State Park, turn around and go back south. Twenty miles later you'll get to Devils Punchbowl State Park. Keep going. Another thirty miles and you'll come to Devils Elbow State Park. Keep going. About forty miles later you'll get there.

Seven Devils Hot Springs, Nevada

This state has more hot springs than anywhere around – 312 at last count. Seven Devils Hot Springs is may be on private property. You can find it on Google Maps, but "soakers" say it's almost impossible to find without a guide.

The Seven Peaks, San Luis Obispo, California

Once, about twenty-five million years ago, this part of the continent was under the sea and experienced major volcanic activity. When the waters receded, the Seven Peaks, or "plugs," surfaced and now define this coastal area. They are: Islay Hill, Cerro San Luis Obispo, Bishop Peak, Chumash Peak, Cerro Romualdo, Hollister Peak and Morro Rock.

Mount Seven, Rocky Mountains, Colorado

The United States Geological Survey gives us the following historical notes: "In 1970, the US Board on Geographic Names approved the name Mount Seven, at the request of the Colorado Mountain Club and to recognize the summit's seven distinct peaks." Unfortunately for all these folks who worked so hard for this name change and for the rest of us septomaniacs, the mountain was renamed *again* in 1984. I don't care for the new name and won't even tell you what it is. Located in the midst of the Sangre de Cristo Range, tucked in the back of the Great Sand Dunes National Monument—a really terrific, unique, fun, and little-known place—this mountain soars 13,350 feet. That's not *big* big, as there are several 14ers around it, but it is a worthy peak and makes a great backdrop for your photographs of the sand dunes. After all, a picture of sand dunes would otherwise be, well, can you say "boring"?

Mt. Seven, Rocky Mountains, Canada

Near Golden, British Columbia, there is another Mt. Seven in the Rockies. This one is now renowned for parasailing.

Seven Devils Swamp, Arkansas

Seven Devils Swamp Natural Area is located along Cut-off Creek at the point where the creek flows from the pine-covered hills of the Coastal Plain to the flat lowlands of the Mississippi Alluvial Plain. The natural area lies within the Seven Devils Swamp

Wildlife Management Area and is co-managed with the Arkansas Game and Fish Commission.

Seven Falls, Colorado Springs, Colorado

A forward-thinking man, James Hull, purchased the land encompassing Seven Falls in 1882: 160 acres for $1,300.00. He was a naturalist wishing to preserve this scenic area, but was an astute businessman, too. He carved a road, erected a stairway, and charged admission. A later owner, Galatyn Hill, added lighting for evening viewing and an observation deck from where all seven of the cascades can be seen. In a state of incredible beauty, the South Cheyenne Canyon ranks as one of the best.

Seven Falls, Santa Barbara, California

Although this is a popular site for a lot of folks, we are told you need to know where you are going in order to get there. The trails are good and the scenery spectacular with ocean views. The best time to go? December to May. After that, you're more likely to find seven trickles than seven falls, as the water gets turned off about that time of year.

Sevens in US Roads and Highways

The Pennsylvania Turnpike has seven tunnels within a seven mile span, and a "seven mile climb."

The north-south highway that hugs the eastern coast all the way from Florida to Maine, I-95, has seven loops designated 295, in Florida, Virginia, New Jersey, New York, Washington, D.C., Massachusetts, and Maine.

"SEVEN" PLACES FROM AROUND THE WORLD

The Seven Sisters

This is a set of cliffs, which look suspiciously like the White Cliffs of Dover, and are located in about the same area on the eastern coast of England almost directly south of London. They look so much like the White Cliffs *used* to (which are now rather green) that they have been used as "stand-ins" for photographs and movies on more than one occasion. The seven are: Haven Brow, Short Brow, Rough Brow, Brass Point, Flat Hill, Baily's Hill, and Went Hill.

You want to hear something really, really sad? The Seven Sisters used to have seven brothers, known as **The Seven Charles**. One by one they were washed into the sea and by the 1850s, they were all gone. We are all sad.

Great Brittan has two other places they refer to as the Seven Sisters – one is an area of northeast London in the Tottenham district. It was so named in honor of the Seven Sisters Road which runs directly through it, and the other is the road which was so named in honor of the seven elm trees which at one time lined the street.

Seven Brothers, Djibouti

This is a group of small islands off the coast of Africa, on the east side of the horn, in the Dact-wl-Muyu section of the Bab-el-Mandeb strait. The strait connects the Red Sea and the Arabian Sea. Perim is the only one of these islands you may have ever heard of, and it is only five miles square.

Seven Sisters, Neath river valley, West Glamorgan, Wales

This small village in the south of Wales is home to Gunsmoke, an old-west cowboy town mock-up for the Welsh kiddies. In Wales. It is also home of the Seven Sisters Sawmill and the remains of an old coal mine. The town and sawmill were named after the Seven Sisters coal mine, which in turn was named in honor of the mine-owner's seven daughters. But who cares when you can go to Gunsmoke. In Wales.

Other Sevens in Great Britain

There are more than just two more places in Great Brittan that have seven in their names. (Quelle surprise, n'est-ce pas?) A 1972 book called "English Field-names: A Dictionary" was written by a man named John Field. I'm not making this up. He listed a bunch of places, and some have such arcane and romantic names that I'll tell you a few: Seven Acre Piece (a piece of land having an area of seven acres or a meadow adjoining such a piece of land), Seven Butts (probably what we would be pronouncing and spelling "butte"), Seven Roods (in England, a rood is a measure of length which sometimes equals a rod and sometimes equals a quarter acre, which is forty square rods), Seven Leys (*ley*, sometimes spelled *leu*, is a Romanian monetary unit and the silver coin of that amount), Seven Day's Math, Seven Greaves (greaves is another word for "copse," which is short for "coppice," which means "thicket",) Seven Measures Sowing (referring to how much seed was required to plant the area,) Seven Halves ("probably 'seven half-acre strips'",) Seven Men's Mowth ("meadow providing work for seven men",) Seven Rakes ("land containing seven paths"; rake can also mean "rock" so perhaps this site had seven stones,) and Seven Shilling Worth, which probably referred to the rent paid for the land.

River Seven, UK

In the far northern reaches of England, over on the eastern side not too far from the North Sea, is a smallish river called River Seven. Contained mostly in the North York Moors National Park, River Seven's claim to fame is that in 1779 Abraham Darby constructed the world's very first cast iron bridge across it at Coalbrookdale. Locals still claim this area to be "where the Industrial Revolution began." The bridge is still there and you can still walk across it.

Important update: This bit about the bridge is just so not true. Thankfully, Katy Whitaker at englishheritage.org rescued me just in time to prevent this otherwise embarrassing mistake. (Someone, and I won't say who, made what I am going to charitably call a typo; the bridge spans the *Severn* River. Good grief, how am I ever going to teach these people how important details are?) But back to my dear Ms. Whitaker. She found a reference to the River Seven published in Doomsday Book of 1086. And you know what? It only took her about five minutes to find that reference. She is very good, and probably should be paid more than she's getting.

Also, for about 400 years, the lands beyond the River Seven were considered a sanctuary from punishment for crimes committed in other regions. Once a criminal crossed the river, not only was he safe from the constables, but his pursuers could be punished for punishing those pursued.

Seven Sisters Mountain, Alberta, Canada

In the Allison Creek Valley at the head of Vicary Creek and not far from the Continental Divide, these peaks rise to an elevation of 8,501 feet (2,591 meters). Seven Sisters Mountain is now the official name; it used to be called the Steeples. First to the summit, in 1951, was Bruno Engler, "with considerable difficulty." This mountain "has seven 'sister-like' jagged peaks," whatever that means. My own sister may take exception to that characterization. Brother, don't people come up with the funniest stuff?

The Seven Sisters, Canada

Don't confuse Seven Sisters Mountain with *The* Seven Sisters, which is a different mountain altogether. It is on the border of Jasper and Mount Robson Parks, on the border of Alberta and British Columbia, on the border of almost nowhere. *The* Seven Sisters is now officially named Yellowhead Mountain, and is only 8,064 feet (2,458 meters.)

Seven Sisters Waterfall, Norway

From atop the high, steep, densely wooded cliffs of Norway's Geiranger Fjord, the snowfall melts and plummets, twisting and misty, to the water-filled valley far below.

Seven Sisters Waterfalls, Cyprus

If you have traveled much, perhaps you have run across a pseudo-tour now and then. This is one of those fun (?) little drives around a place where there is not much to see, but the guide has a witty repartee to keep you laughing so you don't feel duped. The Seven Sisters Waterfall on Cyprus is such a place. The falls are reported to be a small stream that splashes from a low rise onto seven rocks.

Seven Sisters Falls, Manitoba, Canada

There are actually two sets of falls that locals call Seven Sisters: the first is the natural set of whitewater rapids on the Winnipeg River (also known as the Seven Portages) and the second is the man-made set that occurs as a result of the Seven Sisters Generating Plant spillway.

Seven Sisters Falls, Granada

On the island of Granada is another lovely grouping of cascades known as the Seven Sisters. Here, you must hike through tropical rain forest then on through a plantation growing bananas, cocoa, nutmeg and very often mud, to reach the secluded destination.

The Seven Fells of Akaslompolo, Yllashumina, Norway

Not to be confused with *fall*, a *fell* is what used to be *fjell* – Nordic for mountain. These seven, Yllas, Kesanki, Lainio, Kuer, Pyha, Kukas, and Kellostapuli, are in the Lapland of Finland. Not very high, ranging from 718 to 416 meters, you can still ski there. You just won't have far to fall on this fell.

The Seven Fells of Whinlatter Forest, Cockermouth, UK

In England the only area that could reasonably be described as mountainous is the Lake District. Here we find a grouping of seven fells (see above and do not write to tell me about a misspelling again) in the Whinlatter Forest, the highest of which is Lord's Seat at a modest 1,811-foot elevation. Just when we begin to think what a charming term "fell" is, we find Barf is one of them.

Sevenoaks, UK

Also in Kent, England, is the town of Sevenoaks, which now has a population of 25,000 people. Unfortunately, during a windstorm in 1987 the seven oaks blew down. There are no reported plans to change the town's name.

Seven Oaks, South Africa

Here's another town named for a small grove of trees, even though there may or may not be now or ever have been seven oaks anywhere to be seen. When first named, there may have been a couple of optimistic acorns lying around. This place is about seventy-five miles from the east coast of Africa, just northwest of Durban.

Seven Dials, London

Once infamous for slumminess and lawlessness, this historic area on the West End of London, east of Soho, has recently undergone some urban renewal. Laid out in 1690, "as a fine example of French street planning by Thomas Neale," seven streets are like spokes which meet at the hub, which sports a unique tower of seven sundials. Six dials faced out from the obelisk, the tower itself serving as the seventh, making this a masterpiece of engineering. Each dial of course had to be different, since they were facing different directions. It has recently been reconstructed. But we think they used clocks this time. Let's hope the electric replacements also endure 300 years and provoke poetry as:

Where famed St. Giles ancient limits spread
An in-railed column rears its lofty head,
Here to seven streets seven dials count the day.
And from each other catch the circling ray.

The seven streets? Earlham Street, Monmouth Street, Shorts Gardens, Mercer Street, Upper St Martin's Lane, Neal's Yard, and Neal Street.

The Ionian Islands, Greece

The Greeks call this group Eptanisa, or Seven Islands. There really are more, but who are we to argue with tradition? Here are the seven largest, and probably the ones that were counted: Corfu, Ithaca, Kefalonia, Kythira, Lefkada, Paxi, and Zakynthos. They lay in a lovely chain between Italy and Greece in the Ionian Sea.

If you go back in the history of the Ionian Islands, you'll find that in the seven years from 1800 until 1807, the group was a nation called the Septinsular Republic. The Turks ruled the islands during that time, having conquered them with the help of the Russians, wresting them from the French.

Seven Hunters, Scotland

Now commonly known as the Flannan Islands (in honor of the seventeenth-century bishop who hermetized himself there), these seven tiny bits of land off the coast of Scotland have only a couple claims to fame: 1) their existence makes navigation in the waters extremely hazardous, so a lighthouse was erected, and 2) seven men mysteriously disappeared while on lighthouse duty around the turn of the last century.

The Canary Islands, Spain

Tenerife is the largest both in size—2,000 square kilometers—and in population—220,000 residents. It is richly diverse in landscape, having Spain's highest mountain with fertile farms and vineyards in the valleys.

El Heirro is home to 7,000 people. It is the smallest of the islands and furthest west. The terrain is rugged.

La Palma is known for its beautiful black sand beaches and the huge volcanic crater.

Gran Canaria is a haven for tourists, beach combers, shoppers and outdoor enthusiasts, and is the second-largest island.

Gomera is small, lush, forested and quiet. It is the perfect getaway.

Not the largest, but having the longest coastline, Fuerteventura is the place to visit for deep sea fishing and water sports.

Lanzarote had volcanic activity only a few hundred years ago, and the landscape is still lava-black, but beautiful.

Seven Pagodas, India

Also known as Mahabalipuram, also known as Mamallapuram, this island city is about fifty miles from Madras, and is known for "cave temples, monolithic figures, and bas-relief carvings."

Settefrati, Italy

This little town in Italy is wicked old, dating from the third century BC. It wasn't referred to as Settefrati until 991 CE, though. The name "seven monks," or friars, was given to the place by the Benedictine monks in honor of the seven sons of St. Felicia who had all been slain by the anti-Christian Romans. (The seven sons were Januarius, Felix, Philip, Sylvanus, Alexander, Vitalis and Martial.)

Sapta Sindhu, India

The ancient Sapta Sindhu, or "Seven Rivers", was the old-timey name for what is now Punjab, which translates into Five Waters. This tells you what happened to either the size of the country or the fate of the rivers. (And actually, it is both. One river dried up and the area that encompasses Punjab has shrunk so that now only five rivers flow through its boundaries.) The seven were: Asuhi, Purushin, Saruri, Satadru, Sindhu, Vipasa, and Vitasta.

Sapta Koshi, India

This river, which rises in Nepal, is one of the three largest tributaries of the Ganges and the largest river system in Nepal. Translating as "seven great rivers" it starts flowing from the Saptri district and manages to flow rather generously over its banks every monsoon season. Water is collected at other times of the year from glaciers, lakes, melting snow, and springs. Baraha Chhetra is where all seven Koshi rivers meet and form the Sapta Koshi. This is one of the best pilgrimage-destination places for the faithful Hindus, as it was here that Vishnu killed the evil Hiranakshya. The seven? They are: Arun, Dudh Koshi, Indrabati, Likhu Khola, Sun Koshi, Tama Koshi, and the Tamor.

Sapta Gandaki, India

Another important river basin in Nepal is the holy Sapta Gandaki, which is *also* formed from the convergence of seven tributaries. They are the snow-fed Budhigandaki, Daraudi, Kaligandaki, Madi, Marsyandi, Seti, and Trisuli. The meeting of these seven is at Devaghat. Hindus also believe the place where they merge, Devaghat, is a holy destination and a great place to bathe. It was here that Vishnu saved an elephant from a crocodile.

The Seven Isles of Izu, a.k.a. Izu-shichito

These volcanic islands in the Izu Peninsula (about 300 miles from Tokyo) were once used as penal colonies, but now are being touted as *the* hot vacation destination. They seem to have what we all long for: tropical climate, great beaches, a great camellia oil production, and easy transportation from Japan. Those prisoners must have broken all kinds of laws to be sent there. Ah, you want to know about camellia oil, don't you? Well, you're going to have to research that yourself, because I am totally focused on seven right now. I will tell you that it has something to do with anti-oxidants and carcinogen-prevention and neutralizing free radicals. So you can see why I'm not going there.

Seven Mile Beaches

Seven Mile Beach is one of the names that "just sound good" and there are several around, a few of which actually are seven miles long:

Seven Mile Beach, New Jersey, US. At the very southern-most end of New Jersey, on the Atlantic side of Cape May, between Townsend Inlet and Hereford Inlet are seven miles, roughly, of beautiful beaches. Only two small towns, Stone Harbor and Avalon ply to the tourist trade.

Seven Mile Beach, Grand Caymans. "Pristine white powdery sand beckons you to set new footsteps or take a swim in the shimmering aqua waters of the Caribbean." Good PR. Great get-away. Want more enticement than a great place to relax and open a numbered bank account? You'll find 7 reasons here: http://www.tripadvisor.com

Seven Mile Beach, New South Wales, Australia. On the banks of the Tasman Sea, in the Kangaroo Valley about seventy-five miles south of Sidney, lies the wild surf of Seven Mile Beach. Thus termed with no explanation, even though in Australia kilometers are used instead of miles.

The Seven–Star Crags, China

Okay, this is way cool. Langfeng, Yuping, Shishi, Tianzhu, Chan-chu, Xianzhang, and Apo are seven limestone rock formations, tall and straight, that stick up out of Star Lake in the province of Guang-dong, China. When viewed from above, they are remarkable in their resemblance to the pattern of stars of the Big Dipper. Local legend has it that they actually grew from stars that fell.

Seven Heads, Ireland

The recent discovery of gas has been a fiscal boon to this area. The Seven Heads wells are expected to supply up to 15 percent of the Irish gas needs for the next fifteen years. It has also become a travel destination for divers. And the heads? Not exactly what we think: *head* means a jutting land mass. And there are lots of heads in this vicinity and evidently seven in this immediate locality.

The Well of the Seven Heads, Scotland

If you visit Scotland and the Glengarry Castle, you may want to read a memorial plaque mounted beside the Lock Oich spring. It relates the story of a man and his six sons who were beheaded there in the sixteenth century. They had been accused of killing two young boys of the Keppock clan, and were slain for the deed by a vigilante group. After they were killed, the mob beheaded them and washed the skulls in the waters before presenting the heads to the head of the clan. A heady story, indeed. And in Scotland, at least, head means head, not "jutting land mass."

The Seven Men of Moidart

While you are in the Scottish Highlands, also stop by the Seven Men of Moidart. They aren't men, but seven beech trees that were planted near Achracle to memorialize the men who went with Bonnie Prince Charlie on his quest against the English in the 1740s, known as the Jacobite uprising. In the end, they lost and as a consequence, also lost the right to wear tartans and play bagpipes. The punishment for violations was a seven year banishment to any overseas location chosen by the king. (See also the Seven Men of Glenmoriston in the history section.)

7 Site

What became of Amelia Earhart? Many think when she veered off-course she landed on the small island of Nikumaroro, then known as Gardner Island. Folks went hunting for her immediately, and aerial photographs taken in July of 1937 show a distinctive numeral 7 composed of coral debris—probably a natural occurrence. Without explaining why Earhart would write a big number 7, it excited the search party and in 1940, human bones and a bottle were found by a local. By August that year, the British government had sent a party to investigate. They additionally discovered a woman's shoe, more bones, and a sextant box. By February of 1941, it was determined that the skeletal remains had been there for twenty years and were of a Polynesian man, the sextant box was just a box, and the bottle had been lost. Still, groups are determined that with technology available today, better analysis of the artifacts can be made, which will either confirm or debunk Earhart's presence on the island.

Seven Persons, Alberta, Canada

I was tempted to question the population figure (245), ask about their baseball team and inquire about the births and deaths, but was informed that all the jokes have been heard and the locals are frankly just a little weary of them. Located in the extreme southeast of Alberta, about forty-five miles north of Montana and fifteen miles southwest of Medicine Hat, the name was given by the railroad construction crew in the 1890s. They had found seven graves and heard the tale of a battle between the Cree and Blood Indians, in which seven of the Cree lost their lives. "The place was called Kitsuki-a-tapi, which could be interpreted to mean seven persons."

Bommies of Fiji

You can swim with the sharks at **Seven Sisters**, a series of bommies teaming with life off Carpet Cove off Mana Island. Also check out **Seven Peaks**; this dive site off Naigani Island is one of the more popular scuba destinations in an area filled with dozens of them. Namenalala Island boasts another bommie called **Seven Dwarfs**. (A bommie is a wave breaking over a shallow isolated piece of reef or rock located a distance offshore)

Bommies of the Red Sea

The Sinai Peninsula, in the Straits of Gubal, boasts its own set of seven bommies. One, Seven Pinnacles, is a series of flat-topped reefs, known for its colorful coral, leopard sharks and stingrays. Look for this spot using its alternative name "the Alternatives." To the west across the peninsula, just offshore from Safaga in the Soma Bay of Egypt, is Tobia Arba, the Seven Pillars, which reportedly has abundant giant puffer fish, sting rays, and octopi swimming among the soft coral formations.

Telagah Tujuh (Seven Wells)

Reported by a travel guide as a "geological marvel" Seven Wells is a waterfall in Pulau Langkawi, Thailand, where the one waterfall's descent is broken into stages by seven pools. Not surprisingly, there are legends about fairies using the pools to bathe in.

Naam Tok Jet Sao Noi (Seven Little Damsels Waterfall)

Outside of Singuri, Thailand, is another place where a stream kept running after its bed disappeared.

Hill of Seven Colors, Cerro de los Siete Colores Purmamarca, Argentina

Poetically described as a "rocky rainbow," this formation is in the northern part of the Andes located in the Humahuaca Ravine. The Andes mountain range runs through seven countries. Just thought you'd like to know. This kind of information may come in handy someday.

The Seven Giant Canyons of the Bering Sea

The world's biggest canyons aren't exactly where we can all see them; they are at the bottom of the oceans. The seven biggest monsters are under the Bering Sea off the Alaskan coast.

The Valley of Seven Castles, Luxembourg City, Luxembourg

The Eisch River Valley is also known as the Valley of the Seven Castles. The castles are those of Mersch, Schoenfels, Hollenfels, Septfontaines (seven fountains or seven springs,) Koerich, and the two castles of Ansembourg. Some of the castles are ruins, some are private and only the exterior may be viewed, but nevertheless it is a popular tourist pilgrimage to make stops at all seven. And be sure to be there on June 23, as they always have special goings on then.

Bombay

The Portuguese established Bombay as a trading post in 1498 and then gave it to the English in 1661, who leased it to the British East India Company for many years and not much money. The city is actually seven small islands—but only at high tide. This counts as a seven-thing. Trust me on this.

The Copper Canyon, Mexico

The Copper Canyon is actually seven canyons. The Copper Canyon region surpasses that of the Grand Canyon in size and depth and equals it in grandeur. This 10,000-square-mile canyon system, reported to be seven times larger than the Grand Canyon, holds the second- and third-deepest canyons in North America: the Urique and the Rio Verde.

Carved by volcanic eruptions, earthquakes and erosion: Urique Canyon has a depth of 6,136 feet, Copper Canyon is 5,770 feet deep, Sinforosa Canyon 6,002 feet, Guaynopa Canyon 5,313 feet, Batopilas Canyon 5,904 feet, and then there are two others we don't talk about.

Seven Caves

In many South American countries, the origin of man has a similar story and similar spot. The Mayans called it Tulan Suywa, which is translated "Seven Caves." Chicomoztoc is what the Aztecs knew as Seven Caves, literally, but it is also "seven herons" or wombs, which may be similar to the North American tradition of babies coming from the storks and is at Tula, Hidlago. Or perhaps the location is not really known. Around the year 1111, the Mexica emerged from Chicomoztoc to surface at Aztlan, but because they cut down the sacred tree, they were not allowed to stay there. Where is there? La Jolla has seven caves, but "they" don't think this is where.

Sabbath River

The Sabbath River (or Sambation) is somewhere in the deepest, darkest jungles of Africa. Maybe. Once, long ago, there was a story circulating about a river in Africa that flowed six consecutive days, then "rested" on the seventh, then flowed again for six, and so on. Hence it was referred to as the Sabbath River. The odd (odder) thing about the river is that it flowed not with water but with stones. The story is told by Eldad ha-Danite and retold in *Jewish Travelers in the Middle Ages, 19 Firsthand Accounts.* Josephus, the historian, corroborated its existence, but said it *did* have water. As we have said before, good stories die hard. In the 1600s, Eliezer ha-Levi stated that he had seen the river with his very own eyes. He was in India.

Zaganjalka

Zaganjalka is a spring in Slovenia that runs dry every seven minutes. "An interesting hydrological element of natural heritage is the spring Zaganjalka under the Cerkno hill, in the gully Volkova grapa near the Zakrog homestead. It represents an interesting Karst phenomenon, characterized by the changing water flow. At normal flow, it takes seven minutes for the spring to almost dry up and the water to come gushing again from the depths." This is quoted from Danilo, http://vimeo.com/11133721 and there is a fun video so you can watch it happen.

Seven Wells

About seventy years ago R. C. Skyring Walters published an interesting little tome called *Ancient Wells, Springs, and Holy Wells of Gloucestershire.* Therein, he identified a couple of sacred sevens. Seven Wells, near the main street in the village of Bisley, is roofed by a 150-year-old Gothic arched structure from which the waters are guided onto a stone shelf then into a pool. Ascension Day brings the church folk, the vicar, bands, and the village people to the well-dressing ceremony. Evidently, well-dressing was an ancient rite recently revived and well-received by tourists and flower-petal pushers. A well-dressing is a folk art work made by squishing wet clay onto a shallow wooden box and producing a picture using flower petals stuck into the muck. No word on what makes the wells holy, other than their being blessed by the clergy. Perhaps that is enough.

Seven Springs

Just west of Seven Springs crossroads and behind the Seven Springs Hotel, is (are?) reputed to be the headwaters of the Thames. Laurence Hunt, a Brit who has recently visited all these sites, describes the place today as "a large tree-lined hollow ... into which trickle several rather feeble springs. It is certainly difficult to recognize seven distinct flows."

Seven Wonders of the Olympic Peninsula

"The seven landmarks designated as the 'Seven Wonders' are Hood Canal (a deep, natural waterway; home to fish and water fowl), Protection Island (a national marine sanctuary; home to endangered mammals and birds), Dungeness Spit (the longest sand spit in the US), Mt. Olympus (7,965 feet; home of the American Indian god Thunderbird), Tatoosh Island (off the coast of the most northwestern spot of the lower 48), the Olympic rain forests ("the only temperate rain forests in the US") and Grays Harbor ("the largest and deepest natural harbor on the west coast of the US").

India's Seven Wonders:

* Taj Mahal

* Golden Temple (shrine of Sikhs; contains the Granth Sahib (holy book); at Amritsar

* Jain Dilwara temples

* Kutb Minar, "most perfect tower," ten miles from Delhi

* Gol Gumbaz at Bijapur, southwest of Hyderabad, is the second largest dome in the world.

* The Great Meenakshi Temple, at Madurai, the City of Festivals, it is surrounded by nine towers and has 1,000 carved pillars within.

* Khajuraho, Madhya Pradesh, has the largest group of Hindu and Jain temples, well-known because of their erotic sculptures.

India's Seven Sacred Cities:

* Ujjain

* Kanchipuram

* Gaya

* Varanasi

* Dwarka

* Haridwar

* Mathura

Seven Sister States, India

This is a region in the northernmost part of eastern India. The states of Arunachal Pradesh, Assam, Meghalaya, Manipur, Mizoram, Nagaland, and Tripura came together or came apart as recently as 1987. There has been some morphing going on there since 1947, with the states joining and splitting, but remaining distinctive from the rest of India due to their cultural diversity, language, and the predominance of Christianity.

Dzhety-Oguz, Kyrgyzstan

Far up in the Urals of northeastern Kyrgyzstan, there is a dramatic red sandstone rock formation called the Seven Bulls or Seven Oxen. It's a popular place for hikers and is situated on the coast of Issyk-Kul, the "hot" lake, and second-largest in the world, which was historically a way-stop on the Silk Route. Now folks, I've looked at pictures of these hills up, down, and sideways, and just don't see seven of 'em. There are more like nine. So, until we're told differently, let's assume these crazy Kyrgyzs are using some arcane numbering system. Different culture, you know.

The City of Seven Hills

If you believed this is a reference to Rome, you would be correct. It is, but there are a mess of other cities around that refer to themselves as the City of Seven Hills. Ernest L. Martin has been doing some research on the subject of building cities on seven-hilled spots, and he says, "What we observe is the fact that the ancients symbolically looked on the various capitals of the world as having 'Seven Hills.' The significance of this fact even has a meaning for the apostle John who … wrote the Book of Revelation. We find that the last world capital would be 'Mystery Babylon' and that it would have 'seven mountain' (Revelation 17:9) associated with it."

Margaret Manning, author of *Seven: Occurrence of Seven in Religion, Mythology, Science, & History,* has identified thirty-three cities as having been built on seven hills. Wikipedia lists 27, 43, 48, 51 (all those wonderful people who contribute just keep finding more all the time and I have to keep checking back in). Some were overlaps, and neither list names some of the cities I found. Here is my latest list:

San Ignacia, Belize	Macao City, Macao*
Rio de Janeiro, Brazil	Antananarivo, Madagascar
Olinda, Brazil*	Chisinau, Moldova*
Plovdiv, Bulgaria*	Bergen, Norway*
Yaound'e, Cameroon	Lisbon, Portugal*
Peterborough, Canada	Bucharest, Romania*

Guangzhou, China*
Valparaiso, Chile
Prague, Czech Republic*
Bath, England
Bristol, England
Cambridge, England
Sheffield, England
Torquay, England
Besancon, France*
Nimes, France*
Bamberg, Germany
Arta, Greece
Athens, Greece*
Mytilini, Greece*
Kaposv'ar, Hungary*
Veszpr'em, Hungary
Chennai, India
Thiruvananthapuram, India*
Jerusalem, Israel*
Rome, Italy*
Siena, Italy
Amman, Jordan*
Rezekne, Latvia
Telsai Town, Lithuania*
    *capital city

Iasi, Romania
Tulcea, Romania
Kazan, Russia*
Moscow, Russia*
Edinburgh, Scotland*
Pretoria, South Africa*
Istanbul, Turkey*
Kampala, Uganda*
Kiev, Ukraine*
L'viv, Ukraine

United States:
Cincinnati, OH
Ellicott City, MD
Lynchburg, VA*
Marshall, TX
Nevada City, CA
Providence, RI*
Rome, GA
Seattle, WA
Seven Hills, OH
Somerville, MA
Tallahassee, FL*
Worcester, MA

Rome. Around 750 BCE, Romulus and Remus, a pair of twins raised by wolves, founded the city of Rome. So it has been said. Proud of the location because of its seven hills, which reminded them of the seven heavenly bodies they worshiped (Sun, Moon, Mercury, Venus, Mars, Jupiter, and Saturn,) they vowed that the city would not stop growing until all seven hills were within its boundaries. They are credited with naming the hills Paletine, Aventine, Capitoline, Quarinal, Viminal, Esquiline, and Caelian.

Sources tell us that it was no coincidence that capital cities were built on seven hills, but it was in fact, totally by design. Since seven was, even before the Christian era, considered symbolic of completion and perfection, the ruler of a kingdom would seek out an existing town with seven hills and declare it to be the capital. If this is a tradition that continued to be observed into the newer world, we cannot say. But check out the number of cities that are or have at one time been capitals in the chart above. We can tell you that most, if not all, of the existing cities-of-seven-hills have now grown past the boundaries so now encompass more than seven.

Moscow. Once known as the Third Rome (ten bonus points if you can name the *Second* Rome), a legend can be shakily traced to the mid-1450s that Moscow was built on seven hills. They may have had some radical geological upheavals in addition to the political ones, because the seven hills are not readily noticeable. Best sources cite the seven as: Borovitzky, Lefortovsky, Sretensky, Taganskiy, Tryokhgorka (really a grouping of three), Tverskoy, and Vorobyovy Gory.

Lisbon. Castelo, Graça, Monte, Penha de França, S. Pedro de Alcântara, Santa Catarina, and Estrela are the hills on which this Portuguese capital resides.

Istanbul. "Istanbul was Constantinople, now it's Istanbul. Why'd they change it? We can't say. The people just liked it better that way. Why did Constantinople get the works? It's nobody's business but the Turks." Thank you They Might Be Giants. This city can trace its history back 2,600 years, making it what could well be the oldest continuously occupied city in the world.

Cincinnati, Ohio. Mt. Adams, Mt. Airy, Mt. Auburn, Mt. Lookout, Mt. Washington, Price Hill and Walnut Hill are unofficially the seven, a fact that would be disputed by most natives not only for the naming of the seven but also for the fact that they can't seem to really be seen, or that there are many more than seven, or that ...

Rome, Georgia. Col. Daniel Mitchell won the 1834 name-our-new-city contest. Tower Hill, Old Shorter Hill, Lumpkin Hill, Blossom Hill, Jackson Hill, Mount Aventine, and Myrtle Hill are the seven hills that were the inspiration for his suggestion.

Rio de Janeiro. Not only is the city on you-know-what, its population can be said to be seven million people. Read more about Rio de Janeiro in the section about the Seven Natural Wonders of the World.

Thiruvananthapuram, India. One nickname is never enough, so they are also known as "The City of the Sacred Snake" which, in English at least, has nice alliteration. It is the capital of Kerala, and is also reputed to be established on seven hills, a task made more difficult because the reported elevation is "sea level." The hills, if they do indeed exist, have elusive names that I have been unable to find.

Macao City, Macao. How much more can we say? Another city built on seven hills. They are: Penha Hill, Monte, Guia Hill, and four others.

Nevada City, California. Now here is a city with *real* hills. Rather more than seven, actually. So exactly which seven are *the* seven? For lack of official word, we shall abide by the list given by the good folks writing Goldrushcronicals.com: Piety, Aristocracy, Prospect, Lost, Cement, Wet, and American. If I had nothing better to do than research for a book, I'd like to find out about Cement Hill. Founded during the California gold rush, this scenic town was once the third-largest in the state, with plenty of rich, happy, and lofty miners.

Lynchburg, Virginia. At an elevation of 795 feet, this city was hard-pressed to find a nickname, and somehow chose the City of Seven Hills. It sits on the edge of the Blue Ridge Mountains in the central part of the state along the James River and is truly a beautiful city. Even if their Quaker ancestors had an odd conception of "hill." (In fairness, the city website opines that the moniker is in reference to the seven neighborhoods within the town limits: College, Daniel's, Diamond, Federal, Franklin, Garland, and White Rock Hill.)

Tallahassee, Florida. Talk about reaching. Can you believe that Tallahassee is referred to as the City of Seven Hills? The Seven Hills Regional User Group (known as SHRUG) says that the city was established in 1823 on a hill and that they made seven roads leading into the heart of town, so that from whatever direction you came, you had to go up hill. Those crazy Floridians. Makes you wonder what the users group has been using, doesn't it? I think I'm going to stop looking for other cities of seven hills, as things are getting a little ridiculous.

Other Seven Hills

Sevenhill. In the geographic center of the Clare Valley, about eighty miles north of Adelaide, Australia, is a place settled by Austrian Jesuits in 1848 as an awesome place to grow the grapes to be made into altar wine. They were correct, and their wine is so good they are still in business commercially, selling as the Sevenhill Cellars. Sevenhill was chosen as a name in honor of the seven hills of Rome. (See also chapter 3, "Commerce and Recreation.")

The Seven Summits

Each one of the "seven" continents have been designated as having a highest peak, and many mountain climbers have as a goal to climb each one.

Africa has Kilimanjaro, one of the most beautiful and most accessible to climb, having many trails to the top. Located entirely within Tanzania, it is a group of three long-extinct volcanoes, rising to an altitude of 19,340 feet. Two of the summits, Maw Enzi (the lowest) and Kibo (the highest) are joined by a saddle that is seven miles long. Kilimanjaro National Park opened in 1977.

Europe's highest peak is Elbrus. Ever heard of it? You can pronounce it el' broos, if you will. At 5,642 meters, it is *big*. Okay, I am making fun, so I'll translate to feet: 18,481. Don't feel up to walking? Don't despair; they have a cable car running to the top. But this is in Georgia, so sometimes it is not running.

Oceania's Mount Carstensz is a group of peaks in central New Guinea's Nassau Mountains. They rise to a very respectable 16,400 feet above sea level.

Asia is home to Mount Everest in the Himalayan range. A giant in a land of giants, most folks argue this is the world's highest peak. It peaks at 29,029 feet.

The native Athabascans of Alaska boast Denali (meaning "the high one") as the highest peak in North America. You may know it as Mt. McKinley, but perhaps 100 years of that name has been long enough. The state of Alaska has already changed it back to the original. Well, that's not the whole truth despite what you may run across on the Internet. Actually, it is only the national *park* that changed back to the name Denali. But that's not the whole truth, either, because really, the original park was *incorporated* into Denali National Park and Preserve in 1980. And the National Park Service says so. Its height of 20,320 feet is status enough, but this is also one of the most hostile environments encountered on earth as the altitude, latitude and wind velocity combine.

In South America on the border of Chili and Argentina, you can hike about four miles (7 kilometers) to the top of Aconcagua. Man first made it to the top in 1897, and it is rated also the highest peak in the Americas. Its altitude is 22,831 feet.

At 16,067 feet, Vinson Massif towers above the already highest continent, Antarctica. (And don't pretend that you knew that, for heaven's sake. Do any of us know that?) Unknown until spotted by a passing Navy jet in 1957, it was named for a congressman from Georgia (the one in the US, not what used to be an SSR in Russia) and was first successfully climbed in 1966.

Chapter 5

RELIGION

THIS CHAPTER EXPLORES the sanctity with which the number seven is held by so many of the world's religions. Jews, Christians, Muslims, Taoists, Buddhists, Hindus, even Mayans and native American tribes ascribe seven as being divine, sacred and holy.

Actually, I have yet to find a major religion anywhere that does not, to at least some degree. Once again, this is not something from the ages past, but rather seven is heavenly even today.

The Holy Bible

Some or all parts of the Holy Bible are used as scripture by Jews, Christians, and Muslims, so I will not separate it by who-reads-what. The point here is that seven is known as a sacred number and is mentioned 397 times in the King James version and the ordinal "seventh" appears another 115 times. And, no, I didn't count them myself, (there's an app for that) but relied on several sources that evidently did. And, yes, I am aware that other translations have even higher counts. If you care to have the list of all 397 mentions, by chapter and verse, kindly send a self-addressed-stamped-envelope along with a check for $628.52, and I'll make sure to get it to you just as soon as the spirit moves me.

Creation, according to the Bible, was accomplished in seven days, a concept espoused by all three of the religions using these scriptures and one that would continue to influence behavior, business, government and commerce for centuries. This is why we get Sundays (or Saturdays) off. God took a break and told us to also. If you ever wish to make a bet with a fundamentalist, or anyone who swears they take the Bible literally, here's a quote: "On the seventh day, God finished his work" (Gen 2:1-3). So if anyone says God rested on the seventh day, they are only partly correct, since he worked *then* rested.

Here's another little fact that is going to win you one of those bar bets, unless, of course, a couple million people buy this book and know it already: How many of each kind of animal did God tell Noah to park in his ark? You can probably figure out by now that it wasn't two as we usually think, but rather *seven pairs* of each! Technically, He asked for seven pairs of each kind of *clean* animal and seven pairs of each kind of *bird*, but you can look it up and get the details (Gen 7:2-3).

When all the animals and all of Noah's family were finally in the ark, they sat for seven days before the rains began. When the rains ended, God sent forth a rainbow as a sign that He wouldn't do that again. The rainbow had seven colors.

And while we are on the story of Noah and his ark, remember God telling him how big to make the thing? And gave the dimensions in cubits? Have you always wondered how big a cubit is? Here's the answer, friends and neighbors: a cubit is equal to seven palms. So now as soon as you figure out how big a palm is....

Also in Genesis is the story of a dreamy Pharaoh and his visions of seven skinny cows eating seven fat cows. His visions bothered him a lot, and he just wasn't buying the explanations his sages gave. It's a good story with an ending where everyone wins. The Pharaoh got his dreams interpreted, Egypt was saved from a seven-year-long famine, and Joseph, who correctly predicted the catastrophe, won a Get out of Jail Free card and a new job.

The book of Proverbs is another fun chapter, written mostly by old guys giving advice to their sons. Proverbs 6:16 lists seven things that make God really mad: haughty eyes, a lying tongue, hands that shed innocent blood, a heart that devises wicked plans, feet that run to evil, a false witness and a man who sows discord. That was according to Solomon, who perhaps should have been advising his father rather than his son.

JUDAISM

FOR THE JEWS, **Heptateuch** is the term for the first seven books of the Old Testament. They serve as the basis of the Jewish theology and law. They are Genesis, Exodus, Leviticus, Numbers, Deuteronomy, Joshua, and Judges.

The number seven has a special significance in Jewish tradition. It denotes "endearment" and in the words of the sages, "all sevens are dear." "For a Jew ... the seventh day, Shabbat, is qualitatively different from the six weekdays. It is a day of rest from worldly endeavor, a time to experience Divine transcendence. The Jewish seven reflects unity, while the non-Jewish seven represents plurality." Also in the Hebraic language, the word that signifies "seven" means "to make an oath." Even their word for swear (as in taking an oath as opposed to cursing) means "to come under the influence of seven things."

Another source has this to say: "The Hebrew *seven*, consisting of three letters, S, B and O, has more than one meaning. Theirs is a complicated and mysterious language, full of words with multiple meanings and seemingly arbitrary spellings. Near as I can tell, you write with consonants and fill in the vowels as deemed necessary. Ask seven speakers of Hebrew the literal translation or even the spelling of 'seven' and it's likely you'll receive seven answers—none of which would be incorrect. Sheba, or with a soft 'g', sheva, sheh'bah; zaryen (actually this is the word for the seventh letter of the alphabet, but its numeric value is seven,) saba; shaba…. At once, it means *age* or *cycle*, Shab-ang; Sabbath can be translated *old age*, as well as *rest*, and in the old Coptic, Sabe means *wisdom*... it means 'to fill' or 'be complete.'"

Even though God gave Moses ten commandments for his people to live by, the Jewish rabbis of old gave the Gentiles a break and only ask that they keep seven, all the while *encouraging* them to give the others the old college try. It's like the Gentiles must take Remedial Redemption, but Jews are required to study in the advanced placement classes. Both will get the same credits, but the Jews must live up to higher standard. The **Seven Universal Laws**, those given to the Gentiles, also known as the **Seven Noahide Laws** are these:

* The prohibition of incest and adultery

* The prohibition of murder

* The prohibition of theft

* The prohibition of idolatry

* The prohibition of blasphemy

* The prohibition of eating live meat, and lastly,

* The establishment of judicial courts to deal with those who might not be so good about living up to the other six laws.

Each of these commandments has an "inner dimension"—the Seven Principles of Faith and Service. These are sefirot, or emotional powers of the soul: love, fear, mercy, trust, sincerity, truth and humility. And each of *these* is associated to one of seven body parts: right arm, left arm, torso, right leg, left leg, genitals (no not gentiles, we are taking about body parts, remember?) and the head.

The Seventh Commandment

So while we are on the subject of the Ten Commandments, do you think you know which one is the seventh? If your name is Morganstern and you guessed "Thou shalt not steal" you would probably be not be wrong. If you attend St. Paul's Most Precious Blood Academy and answered "Thou shalt not commit adultery," you would probably *also* not be wrong. The answer, Protestants and Jews agree, is "Thou shalt not commit adultery" since that was actually the seventh one proclaimed by God. Catholics, on the other hand, tend to rate the rules according to the relative importance as they perceive them, so not stealing is the seventh for them.

One source also reports the seventh commandment was "once placed before the one referring to killing because at one time adultery was considered the greater offense. In fact, in the oldest Biblical manuscript, a parchment known as the 'Nash Manuscript,' the prohibition of adultery precedes that of killing."

Seven Names of God

According to the *Encyclopedia of Word and Phrase Origins*, the ancient Hebrews had many names for God, but "the seven names of God were those over which the scribes had to take particular care, the names being: El, Elohim, Adonai, Yhwh, Ehyeh-Asher-Ehyer, Shaddai, and Zebaot."

Seventh Day and Year

Time spans of seven are common to the Hebrews as dictated by the Talmud.

Sabbath is the seventh day of each week, the day of rest and worship.

Sabbatical is a seven year time period, the seventh year being the one when God commanded the land should lie fallow and everyone must both forgive and repay his debts.

Jubilee is celebrated, or observed, once every forty-nine (7x7) years as proclaimed in Leviticus: On the tenth day of the seventh month of that year, sound the trumpets, proclaim liberty, and go home.

Seven Blessings, Sheva B'rachot

A Jewish wedding ceremony has a recitation of seven blessings:
The First Blessing is recited over a cup of wine as a sign of rejoicing.

* The Second Blessing thanks God for creating the world. At the same time, it honors those assembled at the wedding.

* The Third and

* Fourth Blessings acknowledge God's physical and spiritual creation of humankind.

* The Fifth Blessing is a prayer for the restoration of Jerusalem and the rebuilding of the Holy Temple, the edifice which so expressed God's special relationship with the Jewish people that the memory of its destruction rises above even our highest joys.

* The Sixth Blessing expresses the hope that the bride and groom grow in their love for each other, with a focus as exclusive as that of Adam and Eve, when there was no one else in the world.

* The Seventh Blessing is a prayer that the time of the Messiah will come to redeem the Jewish people from exile so that peace and tranquility will reign over the world.

Other Sevens in Jewish Life

A shiva is a seven-day period of mourning after the death of a loved one. Shiva begins on the day of burial and lasts through the full seven days. It has been postulated though, that this week is not observed for the sole benefit of the survivors, but because the soul of the deceased hangs around that long, so it makes *him* feel better too. R. Hisda says "a man's soul mourns for himself after death seven whole days." The shiva is observed for only seven relatives: father, mother, sister, brother, daughter, son, and spouse.

Friday evening prayers include the seven principal blessings— mei'in sheva.

A woman will be t'me'ah for seven days after the birth of a son, as she is each month separated from men during menstruation niddah. She observes this self-isolation because she is "unclean" (Lev 12:2). Bearing a daughter makes the mother twice as unclean, because the girl-child is not only mortal, but is a transmitter of mortality, as it were.

Pesach (Passover), and Hag HaSuccoth (Feast of the Tabernacles) are festivals lasting seven days. During Passover, only bread that is unleavened is to be eaten. The Feast of the Tabernacles, besides being a week long, is celebrated in the seventh month of the year. Seven items, consisting of four different plants, are used to make a booth, symbolizing the huts lived in by the Hebrews during their years spent in the desert. Aravan, two willow branches that have no beauty and no smell, symbolize one who does not know God's law nor does good deeds. Hadassah, three twigs of myrtle, which has no beauty but a nice aroma, symbolize a man who doesn't know the law but does good works. Lulab, one palm shoot, which is pretty but has no aroma, represents someone who knows the law but does not apply it. And Ethrog, one citron which is both beautiful and fragrant, symbolizes those who do know God's word and abide by it.

Here are a few more of the Jews' wonderful old wisdoms: "Seven things are hidden from man. No man knows:

* The day of [his] death;

* The day of [Israel's] comforting;

* The ultimate truth in divine judgments;

* What is in his neighbor's heart;

✳ What he will earn;

✳ When the sovereignty of the house of David will return; or

✳ When the kingdom of Edom will collapse."

Seven Characterizations

"Seven things characterize a boorish man and seven a wise man: a wise man does not speak in the presence of one who is greater than he in wisdom; he does not interrupt the words of his associates; he does not hasten to reply; a wise man questions according to subject and answers according to rule; he speaks of the first thing first and the last thing last; concerning what he has not heard, he says 'I have not heard'; he acknowledges the truth." (cited from *The Ethics of the Talmud: Sayings of the Fathers*, translated and edited by R. Travers Herford; New York: Schocken Books, 1962.)

CHRISTIANITY

ONE OF THE kinder, gentler concepts of Christianity is the act of forgiveness. Matthew 18:21 defines the scope:

Peter came to Jesus and asked, "Lord, how many times shall I forgive my brother when he sins against me? Up to seven times?" Jesus answered, "I tell you, not seven times, but seventy times seven."

Seven was the number frequently used to signify a long time or a large quantity, so many scholars would argue that forgiving 490 times was not the point, but rather it was meant that you should forgive countless times.

Statements on the Cross

Judging from the large number of people talking about it on the Internet, there seems to be interest in the seven statements Jesus made on the cross, so here they are:

* ✳ "Father, forgive them for they know not what they do."

* ✳ "Amen I say unto thee, today with Me shalt thou be in the Paradise."

* ✳ "Woman, behold thy son."

* ✳ "Behold thy mother."

* ✳ "My God, my God, why hast Thou forsaken me?"

* ✳ "I thirst."

* ✳ "It is finished."

Seven in Revelation

In the last book of the Bible, Revelation, we read seven letters that John wrote to seven churches. The writing is replete with seven-things: seals, angels, plagues, trumpets, spirits, kings, stars, horns, eyes, golden vials, lampstands, bowls, beasts, heads, crowns, thunders.

CATHOLICS

The Seven Deadly Sins

Ah, the Roman Catholics! They love all things seven, and I know you've been waiting, so here are the seven deadly sins, also called the seven cardinal sins:

* ✳ Avarice

* ✳ Envy

* Gluttony

* Lust

* Pride

* Sloth

* Wrath

The sins were reportedly listed by St. Gregory the Great (one of the Seven Champions of Christendom) as early as the sixth century.

The Seven Cardinal Virtues

To balance things, because there is a virtue for every vice—although the lists are not related as opposites—there are the seven cardinal virtues. Plato, in *Republic*, listed perhaps for the first time these virtues.

* Charity

* Faith

* Fortitude

* Hope

* Justice

* Prudence

* Temperance

The Seven Sorrows of Mary

* The prophecy of Simeon

* The flight into Egypt

* The loss of the Christ child in the temple

* Meeting Jesus on the way to the cross

✳ The crucifixion

✳ Taking down the body of Jesus from the cross

✳ The burial of Jesus

You'll also hear these referred to as the Seven Dolors of Mary.

The Seven Joys of Mary (or, the Mysteries of the Franciscan Crown)

✳ Conceiving Jesus by the Holy Spirit

✳ Carrying Jesus when she visits Elizabeth

✳ Being delivered of Jesus

✳ Introducing the Magi to the infant Jesus

✳ Finding the child Jesus in the temple

✳ Beholding Jesus after his resurrection

✳ Being received into heaven by Jesus and being crowned queen of heaven and earth

The Seven Graces of God

✳ I will grant peace to their families.

✳ They will be enlightened about the divine mysteries.

✳ I will console them in their pains and I will accompany them in their work.

✳ I will give them as much as they ask for as long as it does not oppose the adorable will of My divine son or the sanctification of their souls.

✳ I will defend them in their spiritual battles with the infernal enemy and I will protect them at every instant of their lives.

✳ I will visibly help them at the moment of their death; they will see the face of their Mother.

The Seven Sacraments

✳ Baptism

✳ Confirmation

✳ Eucharist

✳ Penitence

✳ Unction of the patients

✳ Order

✳ Marriage

The Seven Champions of Christendom

I've talked to several righteous Catholics, and none of them has heard of the Seven Champions of Christendom, but in 1596 Richard Johnson published *The Famous History of the Seven Champions of Christendom*, recounting the saints' stories. So who am I to now dispute the veracity of his research?

✳ St. George of England (he was imprisoned for seven years by the Almidor of Morocco).

✳ St. Denys of France (he lived for seven years as a hart, i.e. a deer).

✳ St. James of Spain (he was dumb-struck for seven years over his love of a Jewish woman).

✳ St. Anthony of Italy (he was cursed into a coma and was released by St. George's sons who put out the fires of the seven lamps).

✳ St. Andrew of Scotland (he rescued a bunch of ladies who had been forced to live seven years as swans).

✳ St. Patrick of Ireland (no sevens found, other than he was one of the seven champions).

* St. David of Wales (he, like St. Anthony, was enchanted into a seven-year long sleep).

ISLAM

Seven Heavens

The concept of seven heavens, the ultimate spiritual bliss, is based on verses in the Koran. Muslims believe that Allah created seven heavens, one above the other, and that Muhammad was carried to the seventh on his horse Borak. The higher the heaven, the better. Thus, anyone in seventh heaven is in a state of highest grace. Muhammad reported that the first heaven is made of pure silver; the second heaven is of steel; the third is adorned with gemstones; the fourth is also silver; the fifth heaven is of pure gold; the sixth heaven is made of red garnets; and the seventh heaven is composed of a "divine light beyond the power of [the] tongue to describe." Each inhabitant is bigger than the whole earth, and has 70,000 heads, each head 70,000 mouths, each mouth 70,000 tongues, and each tongue speaks 70,000 languages, all forever employed in chanting the praises of the Most High.

Seven Hells

There are also seven hells: Gehennan, Ladha, Hatorna, Sair, Sakar, Jahim and Hawiyat. Or Jabannam (where the wicked Muslims are sent for a while before being taken to heaven) Lath'a (this is where all Christians remain,) Hutamah (the hell for Jews,) Sair (for the Sabians or Mandaeans,) Sakar (resting place for the Maji of Persia,) Jahim (where idolaters remain,) and worst and last, Hawiyah, the special hell for hypocrites.

Other Sevens in Islamic Life

* Each hell is cordoned by its own gate—hence "the seven gates of hell."

* The Koran defines seven esoteric senses.

* Allah created seven skies and seven lands (Koran 65, 12 and 41,8-11).

* There are seven consonants, sawakit, that are *not* in the first verse of the Koran.

* There are seven towers at Mecca. During a (required) pilgrimage to Mecca, one must undertake seven journeys around the Kaba and seven courses between the mounts Cafa and Marmia.

* The souls of the dead remain beside their tombs for seven days.

* A newborn baby receives his name on the seventh day of his life.

* The Fatiha, the opening of the Koran, has seven verses.

HINDUISM

Seven Tattvas

The Hindus hold to principles or "tattvas" to guide their lives and explain how and why people are happy or unhappy. There are—hold the phone—seven:

* Jiva is the soul or knowledge.

* Ajiva is the un-soul, stuff like time, space, and the senses.

* Asrave is the flowing in, where good and bad thoughts and deeds come in and are turned into karmic matter.

* Bandha is bondage, (the psychic and material kind, not whips and chains).

* Samvar is the stopping of the bondage.

* Nirjara is only a partial release from bondage.

* Moksha is total release from bondage.

The Seven Chakras

The seven chakras are also referred to as "wheels" or "subtle centers." They are:

* Muladhara

* Swadhistana

* Manipura

* Anahata

* Vishuddha

* Ajna

* Sahasrara

Agni the Fire God

Agni was once an important Hindu god. He represented fire in all its forms: heat, light, smoke, from lightening to the burning of energy in one's body to the cooking fire. Not surprisingly, he was red, with wild black hair, seven tongues of fire, seven arms (but only three legs) and seven rays of light shining around his body. Some stories tell of him chasing the Seven Mothers; perhaps he thought a gal for each arm would be fitting.

TAOISM

Sevens in Taoism include:
* The Seven Perfect Ones

* The Seven Perfect Ones of the North: <u>Ma Yu</u>, <u>Tan Chuduan</u>, <u>Liu Chuxuan</u>, <u>Qiu Chuji</u>, <u>Wang Chuyi</u>, <u>Hao Datong</u> and <u>Sun Bu'er</u>.

* The story of retribution of the Seven Perfect Ones

* Seven Day Ritual

* The Seven-Day-and-Night Ritual for Accumulating Merits

* The Seven Purple Chambers of Light

* The Seven Refutations

* The Seven Origins

* Seven Records

* Seven Slips of a Cloudy Satchel

* Seven Summaries

* The Seven Stars

* Secret Merit Stellar Sovereign of the Five Planets and Seven Bright Stars

* Seats of the Seven Heavenly Ministers

If you need more details on any of these matters, I suggest you Google it.

Lao-tseu

It is held that the length of the lobes of one's ears determines the degree of their spiritual affinity. Lao-tseu, the founder of Taoism, is said to have had lobes seven inches long.

Seven Gods of Luck

Probably the most famous, and most-often borrowed, group of gods is Shichi-fuku-jin. You would know these when you see them, their representations are so well-loved and so often used. These funny folks are the Seven Gods of Luck to many Asian households. They are often shown sailing together on a treasure ship and each carries a magical item.

* Daikoku brings good fortune to farmers and carries a magic hammer; he came to Japan by way of China and before that, India.

* Bishamon is the god of war and warriors and carries a magic sword.

* Ebisu, the god of fishermen, carries a fishing pole.

* Fukurokuju is the god of long life, and is shown as an old bald man with a long flowing beard; he is an ancient Taoist god.

* Jurojin is another god of longevity, since one isn't quite enough. This one wears a mortar board and is often followed around by a stag.

* Hotei is the god of happiness. He is very, very fat and is the only one of the seven thought to be based on a human—a Zen monk.

* Benzaiten is the only female in the group and is the god of music. She is depicted with her mandolin; she also came from India and the Hindus, then to Japan with Buddhism.

Other gods and goddesses from far and wide

Archons, Gnostic: those who control the seven spheres.

Chicomecoatl, Aztec: also known as Seven Snakes, this goddess had a young girl sacrificed in her honor every year. She was the goddess of corn and carries the sun as her shield.

Herren-Surge, Basque: a seven-headed flying snake, kept at bay by being fed people.

Pamuri-Mahse, Tukano: This bad boy, only an assistant god, brought a menagerie of some rather beastly beings to earth. One was (another) seven headed snake.

Amesha Spentas, Zoroastrian: Translated as "beneficent immortal", they are gods without being gods and creatures without being creatures. Ameretat, Armaiti, Asha Vahishta, Haurvata, Khshathra Vairva, Sraosa, and Vohu Manah spend their time fighting for truth, justice and the Iranian way. Each of the seven has an archenemy, which are **Daevas**: Aesma Daeva, Aka Manah, Indra, Nanghaithya, Saurva, Tawrich, and Zarich.

Belet-Ili, Sumerian: This goddess was asked to create humanity, so she made seven men to do the work and seven women to produce more men.

Brihaspati, Hindu: He is a priest or Master of the World. He helped create the universe, is the planet Jupiter, and procts the gods with his magic incantations. He has seven mouths to help him and seven rays surround him.

The Seven Gods of Creation, Mayan: The Quiche' book of the Mayans tells of these golds creating man and putting him in the mountains of Guatemala. From it we know the names of the seven: Alaghom Naom, Alom, Bitol, Cabaguil, Gukumatz, Nohochacyum, and Tepeu.

Lamashtu, Sumerian: Oh, my – she was a bad one! This demon was so bad she had seven names and people called her Seven Witches. She stole babies and ate them, killed plants and animals, polluted waters, and fostered disease.

Abgal, Sumerian: These are the seven wise men – Adapa, An-En-lida, E-me-duga, En-me-glama, En-me-gulaga, Utu-abzu, and U-an duga – who attend either the gods or the kings, depending on who you are talking to.

Asakku, Sumerian: This is the name of the seven demons created by Anu, who by the way, was the father of the totally wicked Lamashtu (above.) Their job was to kill off the excess people – the population was getting way too noisy and crowded. We know these warrior gods as Ereshkigal (She Who Wails,) Gugulanna (The Bull of the Heaven,) Hubishag, Huwawa, Namtar, Nergal (Lord of the Nether World,) and Nigishzida. In the Netherworld where they live there is no light, one never returns, and they eat dirt. The Scorpion people guard the underworld gates of which there are seven. When entering each one, a piece of clothing must be removed before proceeding. The gates are: Nedu, Kishar, Endashurimma, Enuralla, Endukuga, Endushuba, and Ennugigi.

White Tara

Avaloketishwara saw the woes of the world and wept. A tear became Tara, the lovely seven-eyed goddess. She represents wisdom and purity, so go to her when you are seeking peace and long life. Finding her eyes is like finding Waldo.

Chapter 6

HISTORY AND GOVERNMENT

WARS. THERE HAVE been more than a few with seven designations. Did they really last seven days? Seven weeks? Seven years? Why do we have seven days in our week? What is significant about bankruptcy and seven? Who were the Chicago 7? What county has seven-sided coins and why? Just how big is a cubit? This chapter answers these questions and many more.

CALENDARS AND TIME

The Seven-Day Week

It was probably the Babylonians who started the tradition of a seven-day week, using the moon's four phases during a month as a guide. This fit in rather nicely, if not perfectly, with the moon's twelve orbits around the earth each year, each orbit taking about twenty-eight days. When the Greeks decided to follow suit, they called the days of the week the *Theon hemerai* or "days of the gods." The Greeks took the names of the seven known "planets," which in turn had been named for their gods—Aphrodite, Ares, Cronus, Hermes, and Zeus—as their guide in naming the days, then added Sunday for the sun and Monday for the moon. They even named the days after planets in the *order* in which they were thought to be distanced from earth.

Interestingly enough, this same procedure was used by Egypt, India, Tibet, Burma, and surrounding countries. The Romans, who used many of the same gods and mythology but renamed them, also renamed their days of the week, using instead Mars, Mercury, Jupiter, Venus and Saturn. The Germanic folks kept a couple of these names, and changed a few for their own deities—Tiu, Woden, Thor, and Freya—which are what we use today but in Anglicized versions.

The Egyptians not only associated each day of the week with a god-planet, but even did so for each *hour* of the day. Using the same inverse order according to the perceived distance from the earth, they began with Saturn, Jupiter, Mars, the Sun, Venus, Mercury, and the moon. Each planet "ruled" their own hour, and so after each seven-hour sequence, they began again.

Seven Bells

The US Navy traditionally divided the day of twenty-four hours into seven 7 watches. The middle watch is midnight to 4:00 a.m., forenoon from 4:00 to 8:00 a.m., afternoon is 12:30 p.m. to 4:00 p.m., first dog watch starts at 4:00 p.m. and goes only until 6:00 p.m., the last dog watch is 6:00 until 8:00 p.m., and finally, the first watch is 8:00 p.m. until midnight.

So far, this is fairly easy. But now an extra amenity aboard ship: they ring bells every hour and half-hour so you can tell how far into the watch you are. So at the three-and-a-half hour mark of a four-hour watch, you will hear seven bells. Since there are only five four hour-long watches, when you hear seven bells it could be 3:30 a.m., 7:30 a.m., 11:30 a.m., 3:30 p.m. or, of course, 11:30 at night.

The Doomsday Clock

Since its inception in 1947, the *Bulletin of the Atomic Scientists* has been featuring a clock section on its cover, with the minute hand indicating the urgency of imminent nuclear danger. Although the clock has not been used predominately on the bulletin's cover for many years, the logo and its meaning remain in the collective consciousness of those of us old enough to remember such things. The design was the brainchild of Martyl Langsdorf, whose husband was a physicist working on the Manhattan Project. She set the clock at seven minutes to midnight, originally just as a matter of "good design." In later years, the clock setting would be used to reflect the urgency of danger, so moved forward and back, depending upon the current world events at the time of that issue.

WEIGHTS AND MEASURES

MEASURING CAN BE done for seven things: length, time, mass, electric current, temperature, substance, and light. As you can guess, over time we have developed all kinds of ways to do all this measuring and all kinds of names have been given to the various quantities.

Units of Time

7 = 1 hebdomad (seven days; a week)

7 years = septennium; septenary; septennate; septennial; heptad

70 years = septuagenary

700 years = septcentenary

(See the glossary for other, longer units of time. Things become seriously long...)

Force Units

Megadyne = 0.1 dyne-seven

Dyne-seven = 10,000,000 dyne (a dyne = 0.001020 grams; it is "a force under whose influence a body with 1.0 gram mass experiences an acceleration of 1.0 centimeter per second.")

Length

Hank = 7 leas (a lea = 120 yards) (this is for measuring *cotton* cloth exclusively)

Hank = 7 skeins

Minion = 7 points (a point = .013837 inches) (this is used for measuring printer type)

Sagene = 7 fontes (30.5 centimeters) (Russian linear units)

Tonde = 7 ares (surface units; Denmark)

Donum = 7 ares (surface units; Yugoslavia)

Cubit = 7 palms (standardized Royal Master Cubit, or Sacred Cubit, Egyptian; roughly the length from one's elbow to the tip of his longest finger.)

Volume

Displacement ton = 7 bulk barrels

Shipload = 7,000 cubic feet (when measuring coal)

Windle = 7 buckets (when measuring wheat; British) (a bucket = ½ peck)

Maris = 7 cotulai (ancient Greece) (cotulai = ½ xestes)

Cyathus = 7 acetabula (ancient Rome)

Viertal = 7 gallons (Denmark)

Adoule = 7 liters (Bombay)

Weight

Pennyweight = 7.77 carats (Avoirdupois weight)

Pound = 7,000 grains

Clove; Brick = 7 pounds

British quarter; Tod = 7 quarterns (quartern = 28 pounds) (when weighing wool)

Bundle = 7 pounds (South Africa)

7 stone = about 100 lbs.

Music

Septimole; septave = "the unit is a group of 7 notes to be played in the time of 4 or 6 of the same value."

Verse

Chhit-ji-a = "a poetic meter where each verse has 7 syllables;" from Taiwan

Septenarius; heptameter = "the unit is a verse of seven feet or stresses, often printed in two lines, especially in Greek or Medieval Latin verse, the trochaic tetrameter catalectic or in Middle English poetry. It may also be an iambic verse of 7½ feet."

Heptastich = "a strophe, stanza or poem consisting of seven lines or verses."

SIGNS AND SYMBOLS

Semaphore

The Navy has a fine way to transmit messages without sound: they use flags. In Navy semaphore signaling, a red-over-yellow square flag is held in each hand and the position of the arms indicates the letter. They use clock positions, but only nine instead of twelve. Then all you have to do is hold one arm in one position and the other in steps around the clock face, except the letters aren't in a nice little order like that. But you can picture the letters being formed by seven circles. The letter Z is the only one in the seventh circle, but there you are.

Since the flags are the same, it's going to be necessary to be able to see the man waving the flags, or you won't be able to tell, say, a seven from a G. The G, which is a seven, is made by the right hand holding the flag straight down and the left flag beside it, but since you need to know if the signaler means a letter or a number, there is another sign that means "number," which must be shown first, of course. I think, although no one has asked, that the flags should be different, maybe opposite, like the right-hand flag would be red over yellow. Then you could really tell if the guy is signaling G or seven.

The website www.boatsafe.com advises us that there are only certain colors that are easily visible while at sea: black, white, red, yellow, and blue. Some of these colors cannot be mixed on flags or they will not be distinguishable, so only the following seven colors or combinations are used for international code flags: red and white, yellow and blue, blue and white, black and white, or solid red, white or blue.

These are the signaling flags a ship at sea would fly to impart information to other ships. It is very hard, if not impossible, to relay information by virtue of a single flag, so even the number of flags flown has meaning. If you see a ship with seven flags flying, they are trying to tell you their position using longitudes of more than 100 degrees. I think sailors around the world must be a very bright bunch to understand all this. Maybe they have special training classes for special people to become designated flag-signal-readers.

Morse Code

Every so often, someone comes up with a really useful, versatile way of doing something. In 1838 Alfred Vail actually developed a code that can be transmitted by light, sound, telegraphy, or by writing. He was busy helping Samuel Morse with his telegraph machine when he came up with this. Morse Code uses a series of dots and dashes and spaces. A dot is one unit of something, a space is one unit of space, and a dash is three dots. Letters are assigned a series of dots and dashes, as are numbers. When you are through spelling out a word, wait seven spaces before starting the next word. C'mon, folks, I know I had to go a long, long way to get to *that* seven, so thank you for your patience.

The number 7 in Morse Code is --- --- . . . Said out loud: dash dash dot dot dot or you can say "dadadididit."

FLAGS

The Bennington Flag

For a rather long time, the United States had no official flag, even though many of the ones flown incorporated stars, stripes, and red, white, and blue. One example was the Bennington flag, which has the thirteen stars arranged in an arch beside and over a big *76*. The thing is, though, all the stars had seven points. Who remembers that?

The Forty-Nine Star Flag

When the United States admitted Alaska to the union as a new state in 1959, for one whole year we had a flag with forty-nine stars arranged in seven neat staggered rows of seven.

Canary Islands

Their flag has seven green stars, one for each of the islands, in a circle.

Republic of Abkhazia

Abkhazia declared itself independent of Georgia—the Russian one—in 1992. The seven stars on its flag represent the historical regions: Sadzen, Bzyp, Gomaa, Abzhwa, Samurzaq'an, Dal-Ts'abal, and Pshay-Aybga. Don't ya love it? They also represent the seven stars of the Seven Brothers constellation. In addition, the flag has seven green and white stripes.

City of Madrid

Their flag has seven silver stars, four over three on a red field. This represents the Big Bear, the city's mascot. The Big Bear constellation, of course, has seven stars.

Jordan

The seven-pointed star on Jordan's flag stands for the seven verses of the first *surah* in the Qur'an, and also stands for the unity of the Arab peoples. Some believe it also refers to the seven hills on which Amman, the capital, was built.

Australia

The Southern Cross in the second quarter (also known as the top or head of the flag) and fourth quarter consists of five stars in a more or less kite-like pattern. The four seven-pointed stars and single five-point star on the right symbolize the Southern Cross: *Alpha Crucis* (7-point), *Beta Crucis* (7-point), *Gamma Crucis* (7-point), *Delta Crucis*

(7-point) and the smaller *Epsilon Crucis* (5-point.) The larger seven-pointed star on the left, the "star of federation," denotes the states and territories of the commonwealth.

Grenada

Of the seven stars, the six border stars represent the parishes of Granada and the star in the center is for the capital, St. George's.

Alabama

The state of Alabama has flown seven flags throughout its history: Spain's (in 1539 when DeSoto paid a short visit,) France's (from either 1699 at the time of the first visit or from 1711 at the time of their first settlement,) Great Britain's (from 1763 at the end of the Seven Years' War when the French gave up their claim,) the United States' (this didn't officially happen until December 1819, when Alabama became a state,) the Alabama Republic's (from January 1861 when they seceded from the Union,) the Confederacy's (during the Civil War,) and the state of Alabama's (since it was adopted in February 1895.)

Seven-gun Salute

Since sometime, oh I don't know, in the fourteenth century, when guns and cannons and things were becoming popular and folks liked to carry them around on ships and stockpile them in forts, it has been customary for those ships and forts or ships and other ships to salute each other by firing off their guns. Firing seven rounds as a salute was very common and considered good luck. The ship's salute didn't just say "hey, we're coming in", it said "we're coming in, and just so you know how friendly we are, we're going to unload our guns so you know we can't shoot at you."

Since the forts could stash a lot more ammunition than a ship, a fort would usually fire back three times as many rounds. That kept both parties even. And that's where we came up with the twenty-one-gun salute you hear about. Sort of. When we say twenty-one -gun salute, twenty-one is the actual number of *guns*, and guns means cannons, not firearms.

Don't confuse this with the rifle volleys shot over the grave at a military funeral. This is done by seven riflemen firing three shots in unison. That's twenty-one shots, but not a twenty-one-gun salute. This is a tradition with a wholly different history. On the battlefield, we used to stop fighting every now and then so each side could go out and pick up the dead and dying from the arena. (We were all very civilized in those days of war.) When a side had picked up all their fallen comrades, they would let the other side know by firing three shots. Then everyone would know it was safe to start fighting again. The military protocol-type folks, then, admonish us from calling this a salute; it is merely a tradition at military funerals.

Bushido

Bushido is another military tradition, a code of ethics of the samurai of Japan. The seven principals of bushido are Gi (rectitude), Yu (courage), Jin (benevolence), Rei (respect), Makoto (honesty), Meiyo (honor), and Chugi (loyalty). Bushido means "the way of the warrior," and they took it *very* seriously. Violations led a warrior to ritual suicide, and adherence to these virtues led to things like kamikaze attacks in World War II.

Seven Directions

Native American Indian tribes of the Southwest have in their culture the concept of seven directions, which are north, south, east, west, then above, below, and lastly, here. The here, or center, represents the spirit or soul within.

LDRSHIP

The US Army has a list of seven ethics that they try to instill in their troops. Placed in the following order, they make the acronym LDRSHIP.

* Loyalty: "Bear true faith and allegiance to the US Constitution, the Army, your unit, and other soldiers."

* Duty: "Fulfill your obligations."

✳ Respect: "Treat people as they should be treated."

✳ Selfless service: "Put the welfare of the nation, the Army, and your subordinates before your own."

✳ Honor: "Live up to all the Army values."

✳ Integrity: "Do what is right, legally and morally."

✳ Personal courage: "Face fear, danger, or adversity, whether physical or moral."

MONEY

Seven-sided Coins

The United Kingdom, in their quest for distinctive coinage when they began decimalization, has been producing two coins that have seven sides, the twenty pence and the fifty pence. Why seven-sided coins? I'm *so* glad you asked. I spent an inordinate amount of time looking this up and would certainly hate not being able to share this knowledge with you now. Round coins are best for vending machines and slot machines and pay telephones—all those devices in which it is necessary for a coin to roll and sometimes then to be measured. So if you want a non-round coin, you will need a shape that is nearly round, has an odd number of sides, and enough sides so that it will roll instead of scoot. Scooting down slots causes jam ups and stoppages, I'm told. And a machine needs to be able to measure the diameter of a coin from whatever angle presents itself. So say you have a square coin, the poor machine is going to get a different diameter reading if the coin settled on its side or on one of the points. That won't happen if you have an odd number of sides, since the diameter measured from one point will end up on a flat part on the opposite side of the coin or from a flat part of the edge over to the pointy opposite edge. Get it?

But the UK is not the only country, or even the first, that has seven-sided coins. So does

Gibraltar; its seven-sided coin is also a twenty pence. It depicts Queen Elizabeth II, as one would imagine, on the head's side and Our Lady of Europa sitting on her throne—a real one, I'm not being euphemistic here folks—on the tail's side.

In Barbados, the dollar coin is one good-looking bit of money, even though it is only made of copper (cheap) and nickel (cheap.) Heads is the coat of arms of the Commonwealth of Barbados and tails is a flying fish. So even if they aren't on a gold standard, or a silver standard, and the intrinsic value of their dollar is not much, I think the coin collectors of the world will enjoy having one of these just because it's so damn good-looking.

And talking about cheap money. . . . Madagascar has a stainless steel ten ariary seven-sided coin. Papua New Guinea has one, too. Theirs has a bird of paradise—the bird, not the flower—on one side.

The United Arab Emirates' sample is a 21 mm. nickel 50 fils. (This reads beautifully in Arabic but loses its poetry in the translation. Trust me on this.)

Mauritius has used a ten rupee copper and nickel coin since 1997. Heads says "The Right Honourable Sir Seewoosagur Ramgoolam KT." So there. And a nice looking fellow he is—suit and tie, glasses, good hair. Probably well-educated, too. The correct term for their seven-sided coin is equilateral-curved-heptagon. Mauritius says so on their website.

In 1980 Jordan struck a coin with seven sides to commemorate 1,400 years of Islam. It is a half dinar with a profile of King Hussein.

Uganda, formerly a protectorate of the UK, uses a seven-sided ten-shilling coin.

The Falkland Islands has also minted a seven-sided coin, another fifty pence. It also has a likeness of Queen Elizabeth II on one side and a fox on the reverse. I guess when you win a war, the loser gets to think about it every time he buys a cup of coffee.

Ah, but the prize goes to ... the twenty-cent euro coin! Produced by the twelve nations of the European Union, these coins are heptagons, but they *also* have seven notches cut into the edge at regularly spaced intervals. Numismatists call this unique shape the Spanish flower.

Seven dollar bill

There was once, long, long ago, a seven-dollar bill in the United States. The particular one I have seen was dated May 9, 1776, and is signed by Josiah Hewes and Andrew Tybout. It is mint green and 71 x 93 mm. It says *"THIS Bill entitles the Bearer to receive SEVEN Spanish milled DOLLARS or the Value thereof in Gold or Silver, according to a Refolution of CONGRESS, paffed at Philadelphia, May 9, 1776"*. The capitalizations, italics and the exchange of "f" for "s" are as written on the bill. The ends state that the bill is issued from The United Colonies and is Continental Currency. The emblem on the front depicts a stormy sea and declares "Serenabit" (which roughly translates "this too shall pass").

Federal Reserve System

The Federal Reserve System is central banking system in the United States. Known as "the Fed," it was established in 1913 and, next to the president, is arguably the most powerful influence in US government. It is responsible for determining monetary policy in the United States. It is run by a seven-member board of governors appointed by the President and confirmed by the Senate, and serve fourteen-year terms. The Fed was founded by seven families of commercial bankers.

Governmental Accounting

All of the funds in U. S. governmental accounting fall into one of seven categories: 1) general, 2) special revenue, 3) debt service, 4) capital projects, 5) enterprise, 6) internal service, and 7) trust and agency. Easy.

Bankruptcy

Chapter 7 refers to the chapter of the federal bankruptcy code that is known as straight bankruptcy. When you file for this, you get to be absolved of almost all of your debts. Dating back to biblical times and traditions, you may file for this forgiveness once every seven years. The down-side is that it hurts your credit rating and is considered one of the most grievous black-marks you can get. Most of these black-marks stay on your credit history reports for seven years. You do not want this to happen.

Presumption of Death

Several federal codes specify that if you haven't been in touch with your family for seven years, they can declare that you are dead. US Code Title 38, Veterans' Benefits, Part I – General Provisions, Chapter 1, Section 108, (b) says: "If evidence satisfactory to the Secretary is submitted establishing the continued and unexplained absence of any individual from that individual's home and family for seven or more years, and establishing that after diligent search no evidence of that individual's existence after the date of disappearance has been found or received, the death of such individual as of that date of the expiration of such period shall be considered as sufficiently proved."

The Social Security Act, Section 205(a) also states: "When circumstantial evidence does not establish the fact of death as the inevitable conclusion, consider presumption of death after seven years have elapsed since the disappearance."

Insurance companies have also used this rule since 1800.

Obscure Laws

Brehon Laws

In Ireland there were, from ancient times until the mid-seventeenth century, four categories of trees, each category being divided into seven types of plants. There were severe penalties for chopping down trees in certain categories:

* Chieftain Trees (a.k.a. the Nobles of the Wood): oak, hazel, holly, yew, ash, pine, and apple.

* Peasant Trees (a.k.a. Commoners): alder, willow, hawthorn, rowan, birch, elm, and cherry

* Shrub Trees: blackthorn, elder, white hazel, white poplar, arbutus, feorus, and cran fir

* Brambles: Who ever knew? Who remembers? Who cares? What difference does it make? I couldn't find these seven listed, I got bored looking, and go ahead and cut me down.

In Montana...

Seven or more Indians are considered a raiding or war party and it is legal to shoot them.

HISTORY

Seven Pines Battle

For two days—May 31 to June 1, 1862—the troops of the Confederacy and the Union fought the Seven Pines Battle, also called the Battle of Fair Oaks, during the Peninsular Campaign of the Civil War. Both sides claimed victory in this Virginia battle early in the war, although both lost badly. Starting with about 26,000 men, many of whom never engaged in action, about half did not walk away. The numbers vary, but the South lost about 980 soldiers, had 4,795 wounded, and 405 either captured or missing in action. The North had 790 killed, 3,594 injured, and 647 captured or missing.

Joseph Johnston, commander of the Southern troops, was wounded and later lost his post per President Davis. George McClellan of the Union army was later recalled to Washington by President Lincoln due to his failure.

Seven Day's Battle

After Confederate commander Joseph Johnston was incapacitated in the Seven Pines Battle, General Robert E. Lee was posted to the command. By June 25, he and his troops defended Richmond in what would be known as the Seven Day's Battle. McClellan, still in charge of the Union forces, "won" four of the five campaigns, but "lost" because, in the end, he still had not captured Richmond. About 36,000 men were lost in the seven days of indecisive fighting.

Seven Weeks War

Just a few short years later, over in Europe, trouble was brewing between the Austrians and Prussians. For many generations, the Holy Roman Emperors of Austria had ruled in Germany, with a few scattered areas of exception. Otto von Bismarck, chancellor of Prussia since 1862, was determined to unite all of Germany. However, Austria didn't care for his administration and declared war, finessing both the alliance of most of the German states and the perception that Prussia was the aggressor. Fighting mostly in Bohemia, the Prussians, under the expert guidance of Bismarck, attacked the Austrians and decidedly won by killing off more than seven times as many of their troops in the short time between June 8, 1866 and the end of that July. Gracious in their victory, the Prussians accepted Austria's surrender and immediately sought their alliance, which soon led to the German Empire, proclaimed in 1871, becoming the dominant power in Europe.

Seven Years' War

Truly the first world war because most of Europe, and later the United States, Canada, and Africa were involved, the Seven Years'

War refers only to those first years before the conflict spread from Europe. From 1756 until 1763 the strong ground forces of Prussia allied with the strong naval ones of England against Russia, Austria, France, Sweden, Saxony, and Spain. King Frederick II of Prussia and Empress Maria Theresa of Austria were in a power struggle and desired the same real estate, while England and France, who just never could seem to get along, jumped into the fray to help suppress the advances of their friend's enemies and at the same time try to gain the advantage of their respective colonial ventures. The Russian/Austrian/French/Swedish/Saxon men greatly outnumbered the Prussian/English, but superior planning evened the score. After about thirty major battles, the conflicts were resolved by the Treaty of Paris, in which the sides merely swapped the different pieces of land until everyone went away, if not happy, then at least happy enough to stop fighting for a few more years.

Seven-Year War

Toyotomi Hideyoshi, a Japanese warlord, was hoping to get help from the Ming Dynasty in China to get himself promoted to Shogun and provide land and labor for his samurai and their vassals. The Ming rulers respectfully declined their help and land, so Hideyoshi decided to take what had not been given. Since the best way into China was through Korea, 160,000 Japanese, armed with rifles kindly provided by the Portuguese, set sail. Their first invasion was a huge success. Soon, though, the superior Korean naval forces cut off the Japanese supply lines. Hideyoshi again approached the Chinese, now with the request that they go halfsies; Korea would be divided north and south between them. Again China declined and decided in fact to help out Korea a little more. In 1593, 50,000 Chinese helped send the Japanese to their knees and far back into the south of Korea.

Hideyoshi *again* went to the leaders of China, this time requesting a truce. The Chinese requested the Japanese kindly become their vassals. Hideyoshi requested the hand of the emperor's daughter. The emperor countered again by sending another 40,000 men to encourage the Japanese to go home.

Negotiations went on and on, all while the Japanese warriors were meeting and marrying the Korean and Chinese women and setting up their new households. "Tens of thousands" of the skilled Korean and Chinese workmen (think Ming vases) were being captured and sent over to Japan. By 1598, the Japanese finally said they didn't want to play that game anymore so went home. The victory of gaining land and skills had been won by virtue of love and marriage.

The Seven Ships

The Acadians, after the war in 1763, were given their leave by the English to return home from Nova Scotia to France. There the Acadians found their former lands occupied by English. In the prior year, France had ceded their North American holdings of Louisiana to Spain. Spain wanted their new lands occupied by their own friends to keep the English away. So after a few years when the Acadians volunteered to go, seven Spanish ships dropped by France, picked up 1,596 folks and sailed them off to the New World world. The seven ships, *L'Amitie*, *Le Bon Papa*, *La Bergere*, *Le Beaumont*, *La Caroline*, *St. Remy*, and *La Ville de Arcangel*, gave them passage, but the Spanish government also gave them money, supplies, shelter, and medical care. The people, who we know now as Cajuns, gave us their unique accents, wonderful cuisine, and distinctive music.

Seven-Generation Sustainability

In every deliberation, we must consider the impact of our decisions on the next seven generations.—Iroquois Confederation

The forward-thinking style of decision-making represented in the quote above is a concept developed by the Iroquois Indians of the northeastern part of what is now the United States. It was their philosophy long before there *was* a United States.

It has also, lately, been adapted by the Greens political party, and quite a few other organizations.

US Constitution

The constitution of the United States can, of course, be changed by adopting new amendments. We've done this many times over the years. Often since 1917, we have chosen to add verbiage to the proposed amendments that allows the various states seven years to ratify them. Before 1917, there was no such time limit, which allowed one, the Twenty-seventh Amendment, to be ratified 212 years after it had been proposed. While that time may be extreme, sometimes seven years is just not enough, which is why Congress once extended the time to ten years in an effort to salvage the Equal Rights Amendment. It didn't help.

The First Ten Men in Space

The Book of Lists, by David Wallechinsky, Irving Wallace, and Amy Wallace, named the Russians and Americans who were the first ten men to leave the Earth's atmosphere. Here are the six Americans and the names of their crafts:

2. Alan B. Shepard – Freedom 7
3. Virgil Ivan "Gus" Grissom – Liberty Bell 7
5. John Herschel Glenn – Friendship 7
6. Malcolm Scott Carpenter – Aurora 7
9. Walter Marty "Wally" Schirra Jr. – Sigma 7
10. Leroy Gordon Cooper – Faith 7

Shorties

* A Lincoln penny has only seven words in English.

* In 1995, to celebrate the Japanese Emperor's seven year reign, 17 runners ran 7,777 meters around the imperial palace at 7 minutes past seven on the 7th day of the 7th month.

* Seven of the United States have a cardinal as their state bird.

* All of the Mercury space missions had the number 7 in them.

Chapter 7

LEGENDS AND LORE

THIS IS ONE of the longer chapters since there are a lot of sevens used in folklore. But this will be a fun chapter and we get to chuckle at some absurd stories we send our kids to bed with and we can groan at many of the old husband's tales. In the section of Traditions, discover obscure laws of Japanese celebrating spring, of old European peace-treaty negotiation, of contracts with the devil and the connection of planets to body part. We will explore the many myths that attempted to explain the existence and placement of stars – from the ancient Greeks to Australian aborigines. Idioms, adages, superstitions, rhymes and riddles. So here it is: a big bunch of hoo-ha!

THE SEVEN SWANS - EUROPEAN

The Death of the Seven Dwarfs – German
By Ernst Ludwig Rockholz
Once there were seven dwarfs living together in a little hut in the Black Forest. A young woman—blonde, no doubt—came by one night and asked to stay. After much discussion, it was decided she would sleep with the oldest dwarf. Soon, an older woman came by also asking to stay. Woman number 1 told her there just wasn't enough room.

Woman number 2 got mad, went away, came back with friends and they killed all the dwarfs.

Quite a charming bedtime story for a youngster.

Seven with One Blow – German

By Wilhelm and Jakob Grimm

(As with many of their other stories, they didn't actually make this up but get credit because they wrote it down.)

This is the story of a small tailor with one great skill, that of self-promotion. When he killed seven at one time, he advertised the fact with a nicely made sash, which failed to mention the deceased were flies rather than men. The implication led him to be feared, respected, and finally to be king. The moral must be "What you don't say is often more important than what you do say," wouldn't you say?

Snow White and the Seven Dwarfs – German

By Wilhelm and Jakob Grimm

For those of you who bypassed childhood or who had it so long ago that you have forgotten, this is the tale of a wicked stepmother/ queen who was so jealous of her daughter's beauty that she kicked her out of the castle. The young lady took up residence with seven dwarfs and agreed to do their housework. As if that were not punishment enough, the queen now wanted the princess dead, not just gone. The plot almost worked, but darned if a prince didn't happen along and revive her. In this "original" version, none of the seven dwarfs are named, and the punishment for the wicked queen was to be forced to put on some metal shoes, hot from the fire, and dance around until she dropped dead. That's harsh, even for conspiracy to commit murder.

The Tale of the Dead Princess – Russian

This is the same fairytale as Snow White, but the evil queen is a tsarina, the handsome rescuer is Prince Elisey, and the seven dwarfs are seven knights.

The Seven Fools – Indian

Seven men were going off to see the Dalai Panaken, the Living Buddha. Along the way, one of them was lost, or so they thought. Many times they counted each other and found only six, since each counter forgot himself. When they came to the Dalai, he counted seven and was credited with bringing the missing man back to life. We are sure he felt no need to explain just how this was accomplished, which made him the smart man he was.

The Seven Billy goats Gruff – German

By Wilhelm and Jakob Grimm

This is the sorry tale of a single mother who left her kids without day care. When the wolf came to their door, the youngsters fought him off as long as they could but finally were overcome. The wolf ate six of the kids whole, leaving only one. Mom returned, heard the sad story from the survivor and gave chase. When she found the wolf, he was evidently comatose, for she was able to cut him open, remove the still-living kids, fill him full of rocks, and sew him back together.

The Seven Ravens – German

By Wilhelm and Jakob Grimm

A man wished that all seven of his sons were ravens, which would just hurry up and leave home already, and so that happened. He must have felt rather silly for doing that, because he never told his daughter about the incident. The neighbors told her, though. She found her bird-brained brothers, turned them back into boys, and believe it or not, lived happily ever after.

The Seven Swans – European

A widowed king had seven sons, a daughter, and a new wife. The new queen didn't care to share her husband's affections, so devised some magic shirts for the boys, which turned them into swans. The swan-boys fled the country with their sister, who soon learned the secret of returning the brothers to their human state: she had to weave shirts for them from nettles, and, while doing so, never speak. Her silence didn't stop her from becoming the bride of a king, and becoming a queen did not stop her weaving. Her new subjects, though, thought she was very strange and probably a witch herself, so they decided to burn her at the stake. At the very last minute, the swan-boys swooped down to save her. She threw the new shirts to them, and they did indeed turn back to human. The only hitch was that one shirt was just not quite finished, and because it lacked a sleeve one of the brothers spent the rest of his days with one arm and one wing.

The Seven-Leagued Boots – European

This story appears in several different versions in several different countries. The boots allow the wearer to take steps seven leagues long. Sometimes the tale says the boots are worn by the giant and when stolen by a mortal, magically shrink to fit—while still allowing the wearer to take the giant steps. Other versions tell us the boots themselves were made from the skin of the slain giant. Often, it is a cat that wears the boots, and then the story is called "Puss in Boots."

The German word for "seven league boots" is *Siebenmeilenstiefel.* In Hungarian it is *hetmerfoldes csizmak.* I just thought you'd like to know that. Some information is just too good to keep to yourself. You are welcome.

The Snake with Seven Heads – Africa

If some old woman magically turned your husband into a snake with seven heads and only you could break the curse, would you? The former president of South Africa retells this story in his 2003 collection *Nelson Mandela's Favorite African Folktales.*

MYTHOLOGY OF STARS

THERE IS MUCH discussion about how stories of striking similarity are recorded in diverse parts of the world. How is that possible? One theory is polygenesis, which loosely says that man develops mental sophistication in the same way and at the same rate everywhere. And because he experiences the same social dynamics—love, jealousy, procreation, fear—and is exposed to the same natural phenomena, it is only natural that people would tell similar stories to explain the world. On the other hand, other social anthropologists maintain the diffusionism theory, which says that a story is first told in one place, then spreads by the natural contact of one group with another. Whichever is correct, and it is probably somewhere in the middle of both, an interesting example is the group of stars known as the Seven Sisters.

Pleiades

Pleiades is not really, truly, a constellation; technically it is an asterism. I am told this kind of stellar configuration is a little unique in that the stars are physically "together" as opposed to several stars looking as if they are together but are at radically different distances and so only appear to be together. It's called an open cluster. Look at all this good stuff you are learning. Faint, famous, and female, people everywhere have told stories of Pleiades, and almost all agree there are seven and that the seventh is often too dim to be seen.

The ancient Greeks named this set of stars in the Taurus constellation Pleiades, and this is how the girls came to stardom: Seven sisters, named Halcyone, Aserope, Maia, Merope, Celaeno, Electra, and Taygete, were daughters of Pleione and Atlas. While old Atlas was busy holding up the heavens (why he is always depicted holding up the *earth* is for someone else to research), Orion the Hunter was busy chasing his wife and daughters. For (you guessed it) seven years they outran him until Zeus, who had condemned Atlas to his fate, took pity on the women, turned them into doves and sent them up to the heavens as stars.

Here are a few of the stories of the Pleiades from places other than Greece:

The Seven Sons of Ishara and Dagan – Mesopotamia

The Pleiades are the seven sons of Ishara and Dagan, Mesopotamian gods. Using magic incantations, the sons provide safety from would-be evil spirits.

Meamei – The Seven Sisters – Australia

This is the story of Wurrunnah, a young hunter who ran away from home after a spat with his mum. On his walkabout, he found the Meamei, or seven sisters, camping out. After stalking them, he kidnapped a couple and enslaved them. Things were going along rather well until he sent them to cut firewood one day. When the sisters hacked their axes into the trees, the trees started growing right up to the sky with them hanging on. Up in the sky, the girls found their other five sisters and decided to stay forever as the stars known as Pleiades.

Another Australian version has the Meamei cast as ice princesses and Wurrunnah as the fire dog who tried to warm them up—or warm up to them, as the case may be. In this version, when the girls joined their sisters in the sky, they never did shine as brightly because of what he had done to them while in his captivity.

The Flint Boys – Navajo Indians

The Flint Boys is the name Navajo Indians of the Southwest give to the Pleiades. According to their lore, after the earth was separated from the sky, Black God had a cluster of seven stars on his ankle. When the people asked the meaning of these stars Black God stamped his foot several times, and each time the Flint Boys jumped up. First to his knee, then to his hip, his shoulder, and finally to his head. Black God thought that was the most appropriate place for the Flint Boys to remain.

The Seven Wives

The Western Mono Indians of California saw the Seven Sisters as women who ate onions. Their husbands were offended, lost respect for the wives, and asked the women to leave their homes. The ladies, suffering from shame and halitosis, wandered off to the sky to become the Pleiades. The husbands eventually became lonely but could never find their wives.

The men could never look up to them when they were home, so didn't think to do so after they left.

Subaru

Subaru means "united" in Japanese, but is also the name they use for Pleiades. The merging of six smaller companies formed the automobile company Subaru, and hence the name and logo. Notice the six stars? Often, Pleiades are depicted as only six stars rather than seven since one is so dim. Not a seven-thing, just an interesting note.

The Seven Mothers – Hindu

The Satapatha-Brahmana holds that the Pleiades are the mothers of the war-god Rudra-Skanda. They are also the wives of the Seven Sages, who in turn are the seven stars of Ursa Major. These mothers, or wet-nurses, were condemned to the heavens as punishment for their infidelity. In some versions, one of the mothers, Arundhati, *had* been faithful, so was allowed to remain until she was sent to Ursa Major as the star Alcor.

Mata-riki – Polynesian

"Little eyes," as literally translated, the Polynesians tell us that Pleiades was once a single star, and was the most beautiful and brightest in the heavens. Tane, the god, became tired of her vanity and threw Aldebaren at her, smashing the one into seven. It didn't bother Mata-riki all that much, though. She decided she was even more beautiful as a set of clones. A healthy ego is hard to defeat.

Ursa Major (a.k.a. the Seven Oxen, a.k.a. the Big Dipper, a.k.a. the Big Bear)

As with the Pleiades, the Big Dipper appears to be formed by seven stars and people throughout the world and throughout time have told stories of them.

Seven Boys Who Turned into Geese – Cumash Indians

With all the classic elements of European fairytales, the Cumash Indians of California tell of seven young men, starving and abused by stepfathers. The judicious placing of a few feathers, a few magic words, and they become geese who flew to the heavens, becoming stars.

The Seven Hunters – Micmac and Iroquois Indians

Both tribes tell the story of the bear—the dipper—being chased by seven hunters. The three hunters in the lead are the stars of the dipper's handle and are visible throughout the year. The following four hunters cannot be seen in the fall and winter months, as they have given up the pursuit.

The Coffin of al-Naash – Arab

Many cultures have seen the seven stars of Ursa Major as a casket, as did the Arabs of old. The casket is the four stars of the dipper, occupied by al-Naash who has been killed by al-Jadi, depicted as the North Star. Al-Naash's children are the stars of the dipper's handle.

Corona Borealis

Greek mythology tells us that this crescent-shaped constellation is the crown given to Ariadne by Dionysus. He felt sorry for her when her husband, Theseus, left her in Crete (whether this was by mistake or by design is dependent upon the storyteller). Ariadne and Theseus had gone there to kill the Minotaur, who had killed seven maidens and seven young men. The hunt was successful, mainly due to the quick thinking of Ariadne, who gave Theseus a ball of string so he could find his way back out of the labyrinth. What happened to their relationship on the way home remains to be seen, but either his ingratitude or her disposition caused her to be left. The crown that Dionysus made for her had seven stars, representing the slain maidens. Upon her death, the crown was placed in the sky.

The Tail of Leo

Ptolemy III set off to war. His wife, who was also his sister, pledged to give her hair to the gods if they allowed him to return safely and victoriously. She cut her hair and left it in the war-god's temple. Alas, the very first night the hair disappeared. The folks were told that the wind carried the locks up to heaven and there became the seven stars on the tail of the constellation Leo and should be called Coma Beren.

LEGENDS

Seven Against Thebes

According to Greek legend, when Oedipus was banished from Thebes, he and his two sons agreed that the boys would take turns being king. However, the younger son, Eteocles, had a good time in his first year and decided he would keep the throne for a second term. Polyneices, the second son, banded together with six of his buddies—Adrastus, Amphiaraus, Hippomedon, Capaneus, Tydeus, and Parthenopaeus—to overthrow the bro. Attacking one of Thebes's seven gates, the battle was a tie, so they had a sudden-death extra inning between the two sons, who promptly killed each other. The remaining six heroes soon became five martyrs, as they couldn't fight as well as they hoped. The seven sons of the sole survivor continued the war.

Seven Sleepers of Ephesus

Ephesus was a town in what is now Turkey. Long ago, Decius, a mean-spirited heathen, was making good on his efforts to suppress Christianity in his empire. Seven men—Maximillian, Jambichos, Martin, John, Dionysios, Exakostodianos, and Antoninos (the names vary according to the teller and his proclivities)—were tried, found guilty, and sentenced to death. They went into a cave to pray but were found, and Decius had a stone rolled over to block the cave entrance to prevent them from leaving. The men fell asleep and woke up the next morning to find several centuries had passed, that the land was now Christian, and they had been canonized. As an honored and holy place, a huge church was built over the cave entrance, and each year a feast is held in remembrance of the miracle. (Ephesus's other claim to fame is the Temple of Artemis, one of the seven ancient wonders of the world.)

This legend is repeated in Jewish and Islamic lore, as well as in various countries of Europe, Asia, including India. If you notice a theme similar to Washington Irving's *Rip Van Winkle,* you would not be alone.

The Seven Viziers (a.k.a. the Seven Sages, a.k.a. the Seven Wise Masters, a.k.a. Sinbadnameh) – Indian, Middle-Eastern

An old king once sent his son to school under the tutelage of Sinbad (not the sailor, the other one). As part of the education, Sinbad told the prince to sit down and shut up. It was during this quiet time out that the student's stepmother tried to take advantage of the young man. Caught, she tried to talk her way out of things, telling seven stories of how she was the seduced rather than the seducer. Each story was knocked out of court by the king's seven wise men, who countered each tale with one of the evil uses of feminine wiles.

To date, I have found sixty-six versions of this same story, proving the popularity of its theme.

The Seven Hathors – Egyptian

For reasons lost to antiquity, these seven figures are depicted either as lovely ladies or as cattle. Also lost is the history of the Hathor's transformation from one deity into seven. *Hathor* is actually the Greek spelling of *Het-Hert,* loosely translated in English as "the house above," as she/they were goddesses of the sky.

When human, the Seven Hathors were found at the birth of babies, where it was their job to pronounce the newborn's fate. Using the red ribbons from their hair, they would tie up the evil spirits and keep the kids from doing dastardly deeds.

They are known by various names, and you will find references to these ladies in the Mythological Papyrii, the Book of the Dead, and depicted in the tombs of Egyptians such as Queen Nefertiti.

Seven Death – Mayan

Popol Vuh is one of the earliest written manuscripts from the Mayans of Guatemala. Transcribed into English in the mid-1500s, it is a collection of stories of god-heroes before man came into being. Two of the most prominent heroes were the twins One Hunahpu and Seven Hunahpu. They played a game like soccer but chose as their playing field the area directly above Xibalba, the underworld home of One Death and Seven Death. The Death men lured the two Hunahpus down for a game but insisted they come the evening before to spend the night in the Dark House. Our two heroes did not survive their stay. Even so, one of them was able to conceive another set of twins with Blood Woman when his disembodied head managed to spit on her. These sons were more successful in their dealings with One Death and Seven Death, and went on to fight other evil gods. Their most challenging foe was Seven Macaw, a bird who claimed to be the sun and moon.

The Seven Cities of Gold – North American

This could well be the neatest trick for getting a bunch of marauders to haul ass out of town: leak the greedy guys a few vague but believable facts concerning huge riches for the taking just a few hundred miles away. The Aztecs, eager to be rid of Cortez and his gang, may have done just that in the 1520s. Seven good Spanish bishops had reportedly established the cities as a place to stash their cash when the Moors had been harassing *them* in *their* country. (Some report that the bishops fled to the legendary Island of Seven Cities, a place that many have found but from where none have returned.)

Perhaps the story started with Cabeza de Vaca and the place he called Cibola. He had lost his ship and then his way and wandered around with his men, arriving finally with stories of sightings of the cities. Soon, Fray Marcos de Niza took a trip up north and, whadaya know, he saw the cities too! This led Coronado on an expedition of his own in the 1540s. Needless to say, Coronado never found the seven cities but blamed it on bad reporting by de Niza's group. He continued to believe in their existence, as they were told by Indians along the route, "Yep, the cities are just up the road there a bit." They got as far as northern Kansas before they found Quivera, but still no gold.

A good story just won't die. In New Mexico even today, there are those who choose to believe there are seven caves where gold was mined and traded to the Aztecs. (Those wishing a map to this site may wire their liquidated IRAs to my agent and arrangements will be made forthwith to get you the copy.)

The Seven Steps – German

Long ago, two neighboring farmers became embroiled in a property-line dispute. One was sure the other was farming just a little over the line. The defendant swore this was not true and so off to court they went. Actually, the court came to them to view the scene of the crime. Unable to tell just whose plow had turned the soil, again the accused farmer protested he was innocent, saying, "May God strike me dead before I take the seventh step if I am in the wrong" and walked off. On his seventh stride, however, he vanished. The footsteps turned to stone and are said to remain until this day near the town of Eberloh.

The Seven Bulls – Kyrgyzstani

Far up in the mountains of Kyrgyzstan there lived two khans who were feuding. The evil one of the two kidnapped the other's beautiful wife. When her return was demanded, the sage advisors of the evil-doer came up with the following plan: send her back—dead. That would comply with the demand, yet save face. Sounding like a fine idea, the wicked khan arranged for an elaborate pre-sacrificial celebration for his tribesmen to be held up in the mountains. Seven red bulls were brought to be slaughtered for the barbeque. When this had been done, the khan himself killed the rival's bride, spilling her hot, red blood down the mountains along with the bulls' blood. This stained the seven crags forever, and heated the waters of the lake so that, to this day, it has never cooled.

The Seven Stones of Morin – German

These seven stones, still standing, are said to be the remains of the young men who urinated on their picnic lunch. Why that would be a crime punishable to this degree is something only the Germans could tell.

The Seven Whistlers – English

The English, mainly sailors and miners, are said to fear the appearance of a flock of seven plovers, otherwise known as whistlers. Usually appearing at night, they are an omen of dreadful things to come. Their ghostly appearance and eerie calls portend even death to those who encounter them. Even the sighting of *six* is bad news, for they are in search the seventh, and when he is found, the end of the world is sure to follow.

If that isn't dire enough, it was believed that the seven whistlers were the souls of either drowned fishermen or, worse yet, of unbaptized babies destined to fly the skies for eternity.

William Wordsworth speaks of the Seven Whistlers in "Though Narrow Be that Old Man's Cares."

Of high astonishment and pleasing fear.

He the seven birds hath seen, that never part,

Seen the seven whistlers in their nightly rounds,

And counted them: and oftentimes will start—

For overhead are sweeping Gabriel's hounds

Doomed, with their impious Lord, the flying Hart

To chase forever, on aerial grounds!

The Seven Voyages of Sinbad

This tale actually has two characters named Sinbad—one was a wealthy merchant and the other a lowly old servant. (If the story bears a striking resemblance to Homer's Odyssey, it is not because the authors knew each other, but more likely they had each heard the same legends.) Sinbad the Sailor describes to Sinbad the Porter just how he went to seek his fortune and found it. On each of the journeys he encounters grave danger that was overcome. They were as follows: 1) he mistook a whale for an island, 2) he took a ride on a roc, 3) he messed around with a Cyclops, 4) he married a foreigner without knowing local customs, 5) he out-foxed Old Man, 6) he went mountain climbing, and 7) he became a slave of pirates.

The Odyssey – Homer

Here you will read very much the same stories as in *Sinbad*, but one character in particular deserves special mention in the book of sevens: the minotaur. He was a creature composed of the lower part of a man and the torso of a bull. It was his wont to eat seven little boys and seven little girls once every seven years.

TRADITIONS

Seven Grasses, or **Nanakusa** – Japanese

On January 7 each year, the Japanese traditionally eat a hearty rice soup called *nanakusa-gayu*, made with the first seven herbs (grasses? vegetables?) that sprout in the spring. (Perhaps their seasons are slightly different from the ones in the West?) It is thought this meal will ward off evil and encourage good health throughout the year. They call the seven plants of spring *haru non nanakusa*. Although the combination varies according to area, they are most often *seri* (parsley), *nazuna* (shepherd's purse), *hahakogusa* (cottonweed), *akobe* (chickweed), *hotokenoza* (bee nettle), *kabu* (turnip), and *daikon* (radish). I have it on good authority that the grocery stores package these all together to make things simple for today's cooks.

The autumn is also celebrated with seven herbs, or *aki no nanakusa*, but these plants are used for decorating rather than eating. And what a delightful bouquet they will make: *hagi* (bush clover), *kikyou* (bellflower), *ominaeshi* (looks something like a yellow status), *fujibakama* (translates to something like "purple pants"), *obana* (pampas grass), *nadeshiko* (pinks) and *kuzu* (arrowroot.) Leave it to those creative Japanese to make this work as something attractive. Or maybe that isn't the point at all.

Hindu wedding ceremonies, *Sapthapathi*, are rife with sevens. The bridegroom must walk seven times around the holy fire, helping the bride to take seven steps. With each step the groom recites a mantra to his bride, asking Vishnu to bless her with seven things:

* Unlimited food

* Excellent health and boundless energy

* Performing her rituals throughout her life

* Giving her happiness

* Making her livestock produce and reproduce

* Making all the seasons beneficial

* Making all her sacrifices to the holy fire successful

La Bigilia – Italy

A time-honored religious tradition of Italians is to fast for the day proceeding Christmas Eve, then feast on a meal of seven different sea foods. If the seven fish represent the seven sacraments, the seven gifts of the Holy Spirit, or the fact that seven of the apostles were fishermen is not clearly remembered.

Seven Sweets and Seven Sours - Dutch

Dutch women, at least those who we refer to as Pennsylvania Dutch and their close neighbors the Amish, are famous for their cooking and the abundance of their mealtime spreads. It is customary for them to serve "exactly" seven sweet things and seven sour things at their tables. Maybe they are just trying to use up all the things they so carefully grew, then had to pickle, pectin-ate, preserve, can, cure, coddle, spice and spoof up. So, you may expect to see pickled cucumbers, eggs, cabbage and pears along with jams, jellies, and butters made from peaches, apples, cherries, pears, strawberries, and rhubarb, then chow, tomato aspic, applesauce, gingered tomatoes, spicy beets – whatever. Getting hungry yet?

Double Seven Day, a.k.a. the Night of Sevens, a.k.a. Seventh Sister's Birthday – China

Also known as Lover's Day, or *Qi Qiao Jie*, the seventh day of the seventh moon (which is Ghost's month) is celebrated much as our Valentine's Day. A bittersweet story of two lovers turned into stars is the tale that serves as its basis: A man, Miulang, stole the clothes of Zhinu, a goddess, which, for reasons unknown, endeared the farmer to her. The in-laws became involved and separated the couple, turning them into stars—Miulang became Altair and Zhinu is Vega—and allowing them to meet only once every 100 years.

Weddings in Iran

A curtain separates the man and woman during an Iranian wedding ceremony. They join hands and have them tied together with a long cord wrapped seven times around the hands, seven times around the couple, and seven times around the knot again.

Birthdays in Nepal

Stanley Sturges, a physician who spent many years in Nepal and wrote *In the Valley of 7 Cities*, describes the following Buddhist tradition of Janko he observed there:

> *Age carries respect, and when an individual reaches the ripe old age of seventy-seven years, seven months, and seven days, he is honored by the entire village. The ceremony consists of placing the honoree in a small wooden-wheeled cart and pulling him through the length of the village with all his relatives preceding, dressed in their finery, and from thence to the feast. It seemed something like a golden wedding anniversary ... with the old ... sensing the warmth and affection of friends and neighbors. [33]*

Births and Deaths - Japan

Japanese celebrate a birth on the seventh day; they mourn their dead on the seventh day and the seventh week after the passing.

Feng Shui

The ancient tradition of using Feng Shui to manipulate your environment to your best interest also observes the number seven. In her book *Fung Shui for the Classroom*, Debra Keller advises teachers to keep the following seven items in the classroom in order to promote effective learning:

* bamboo for inner strength

* a dragon for good luck

* a turtle for patience

* a dolphin for intelligence

* a globe for curiosity

* a phoenix for opportunity, and

* orchids for bravery.

*

IDIOMS

24/7 – meaning all the time, as in 24 hours a day, seven days a week (in the UK, this is 7/24)
a seven day's wonder – something too good to be true; miraculous
at sixes and sevens – not agreeing with, stalemated; also, confused, trying to do the impossible
in seventh heaven – euphoric, at an emotional high
knock seven bells out of – give someone a beating (old naval term)
seven come eleven – a wish for good luck (probably from craps)

do the work of seven mullas – meaning to accomplish nothing
the seven year itch – the notion that marriages are at a low point after seven years, resulting in a spouse having an urge to stray

ADAGES

"**Fall seven times, get up eight.**" (Japanese)
"**Measure seven times, cut once.**" (Russian)
"**If you break a mirror, you will have seven years of bad luck.**" (Anglo-Saxon)
"**If you sing before seven, you'll cry before eleven.**" (Irish)
"**Seven nannies make a child not tended.**" (Russian)
"**Keep a thing for seven years and you'll find a use for it.**" (Irish)
"**Six hours of sleep for a man, seven for a woman, eight for a fool.**" (English)
"**A cat hides her kittens in seven different places.**" (Cypriot)
"**Seven people don't wait for one.**" (Russian)
"**Seven is company and nine is confusion.**" (Spanish)
"**Seven make a banquet, nine make a clamor.**" "*Septem convivium, novem convicium.*" (Latin)
"**Give me a child for the first seven years and you may do what you like with him afterwards.**" (Yiddish)
"**For a mad dog, seven miles is not a [long] detour.**" (Russian)
"**Seven brothers in a council make wrong right.**" (Spanish)
"**The lie has seven endings.**" (Swahili)
"**Seven sets of ewers, but no dinner or lunch.**" (Persian)
"**One must turn the tongue seven times in the mouth before speaking.**" (French)
"**Whatever you do, think about it seven times.**" (Filipino)
"**A cat has nine lives as the onion has seven skins.**" (German)
"**February has seven hats.**" (Corsican)
"**For every one with a plow, there are seven with spoons.**" (Russian)
"**Seven trades but no luck.**" (Arabian)
"**A dead man is mourned seven days; a fool, his lifetime.**" (Yiddish)
"**If he has seven blind daughters, he will marry them in an hour.**" (Persian)
"**A fool can ask more questions than seven wise men can answer.**"

(Italian)

"A handful of good life is better than seven bushels of learning."
(French)

"A threatened man lives seven years." (Dutch)

"Better one cow in peace than seven in trouble." (Danish)

"When we take one step toward to God, he takes seven steps toward us." (Indian)

"Hachi saiku shichi binbou." (Japanese) Literally translated, a bag of
seven works. (Jack of all trades, master of none.)

"From opening the mouth, seven ills may ensue." (Hindi)

"You may poke a man's fire after you've known him for seven years."
(English)

   "Work like you have seven fingers." (Yiddish)

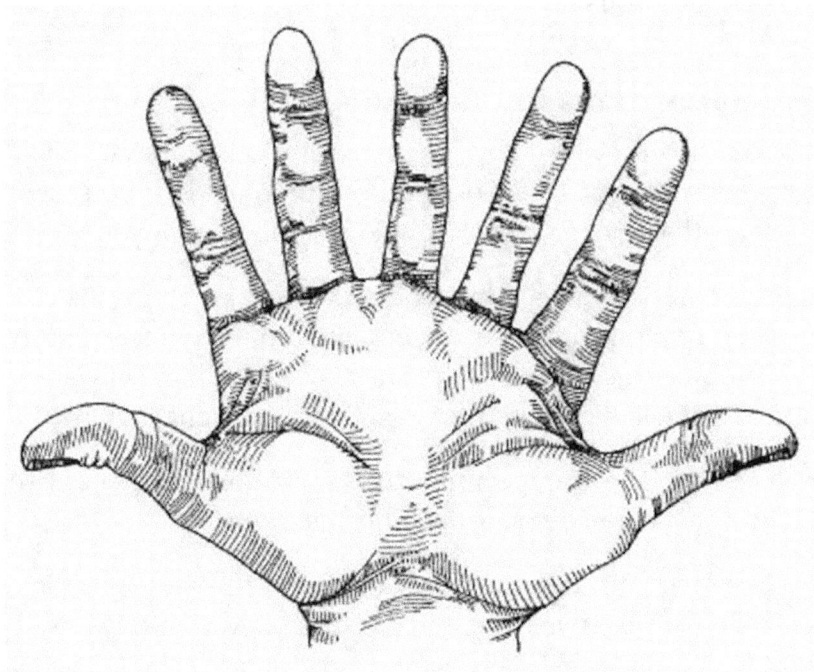

✳

SUPERSTITIONS

The seventh son of a seventh son:

* Has the ability to cure by "laying on of hands"

* Is blessed

* Is clairvoyant

* Can cast spells

* Has "second sight"

* Is doomed to become a vampire (Romania)

* Can cure warts

Other Superstitions from Around the World

* You can cure a wart by rubbing castor oil on it every night for seven nights. (This works especially quickly if you have the seventh son of a seventh son do the rubbing *for* you.)

* You can cure a wart by rubbing it with seven grains of corn, then feeding the corn to your neighbor's chickens. (Do not combine this cure with the one above. It will make your neighbor's chicken gag and that is not a pretty sight.)

* Each day, the average human has seven sexual fantasies. (Actually, this could be true, but who's *checking*?)

* Chewing gum takes seven years to pass through your digestive system. (This is *not* true, and you may tell your mother I said so.)

* The woman who wears seven petticoats will find happiness. – Portugal

* Sterile women should roll their belt seven times around a tree trunk. – Morocco (First find a very small tree or lose some weight.)

✳ If a person dies without having been given the proper rituals, his ghost will return every year during the seventh moon to haunt the living. – China

✳ If you cannot find a suitor, bathe in the ocean and let seven waves pass over you. – Syria (Perhaps bathing in *anything* would help, if you haven't done so recently.)

✳ When seven young women assist in a family meeting, one will marry in the coming year.

✳ The Batak people believe that all plants, trees, fish and animals came from seven eggs. – Sumatra.

A DITTY, a RIDDLE and SEVEN MOTTOS

On sneezing:

One for sorrow,
Two for joy,
Three for a letter,
Four for a boy.
Five for silver,
Six for gold.
Seven for a secret,
Never to be told.

As I was going to St. Ives
I met a man with seven wives.
Each wife had seven sacks.
Each sack had seven cats.
Each cat had seven kits.
Kits, cats, sacks, wives.
How many were going to St. Ives?
– Mother Goose

(If you don't remember this one from second grade, and are doing the math, save yourself the effort and re-read the first sentence.)

Just when you thought this was an oldie, I'm going to tell you how really, really, really old it is. There is a paper by Fibonacci called *Liber Abaci*, written in 1202. Here's how he wrote the riddle at that time:

> Seven old women are traveling to Rome.
> On each mule are seven sacks.
> In each sack are seven loaves of bread.
> In each loaf are seven knives.
> Each knife has seven sheaths.
> What is the total of all of these?

Some folks think he was just expressing the fascination many old mathematicians had for the geometric progression of seven. But maybe he was just doing some school work and came across the obscure writings by Ahmes. Ahmes was an Egyptian scribe who wrote down a bunch of stuff, and his Rhind Papyrus, which dates from 1650 BCE—that's *BCE*, folks—describing some math problems that were already several hundred years old. Here's the way it was written back then:

> A man has seven houses,
> Each house contains seven cats,
> Each cat has killed seven mice,
> Each mouse had eaten seven ears of spelt,
> Each ear had seven grains on it.
> What is the total of all of these?

One would think, wouldn't one, that after 4,000 years this would cease being a remotely interesting little puzzle or that it would still be stumping grade school kids.

Mottos of the Seven Sages of Greece

"Of wicked men the number dothe exceede." – Bias of Priene (There are lots of bad people.)

"Knowe thyselfe." – Chilon of Sparta　　　　　(Know thyself.)

"Keepe still the meane." – Cleobulus of Lindos (Take the middle road.)

"Restraine thy wraithe." – Periander of Corinth (Hold your temper.)

"Nothinge too mutche." – Pittacus of Mitylene (Avoid extremes.)

"Remember still thy ende." – Solon of Athens (Keep your goals in sight.)

"Flee sewertiship." – Thales of Miletos (Take a chance.)

QUOTES

"Nobody can remember more than seven of anything."

Cardinal Robert Bellarmine, 1542-1621

"Crowd not your table; let your numbers be not more than seven and never less than three."

William King, in *The Art of Cookery*

"We've been waiting seven hundred years, you can have the seven minutes."

Tim Pat Coogan, 1/16/1922, when he arrived late at the Dublin Castle for the handover by the British forces.

"Grown old in love from seven till seven times seven, Too oft have wished for Hell for ease from Heaven."

Blake, in *Grown Old in Love*

*

"Seven hours to law, to soothing slumber seven; Ten to the world allot and all to heaven."

Sir William Jones, 1746-1794

*

"If seven maids with seven mops

Swept it for half a year

'Do you suppose' the Walrus said

'that they could get it dear?'

'I doubt it,' said the Carpenter

and shed a bitter tear."

Lewis Carroll, 1872, *Through the Looking-Glass and What Alice Found There*

*

"And the stars in her hair were seven."

Dante Gabriel Rossetti, 1850, in *The Blessed Damzel*

*

"All things were made by sevens in the starry heaven."

Aristobulus, second century BC

"I doubt whether anyone could adequately celebrate the properties of the number seven, for they are beyond all words. Yet the fact that it is more wondrous than all that is said about it is no reason for maintaining silence regarding it. Nay, we must make a brave attempt to bring out all that is within the compass of our understanding, even if it be impossible to bring out all or even the most essential points."

Philo of Alexandria, 20 BCE–50 CE

"Give me the children until they are seven and anyone may have them afterwards."

Sir Francis Xavier

"Let's forget about the six feet and talk about the seven inches."

Mae West

"All human actions have one or more of these seven causes: chance, nature, compulsion, habit, reason, passion, desire."

Aristotle

"Well, her face was so wrinkled it looked like seven miles of bad road."

W. C. Fields

✴

"Madam, there's no such thing as a tough child. If you parboil them first for seven hours, they always come out tender."

W. C. Fields

✴

"Golf is based on honesty; where else would you admit to a seven on a par three?"

Jimmy Demaret

✴

"Essentially, we are a breed of men and women concerned with the arrangement of the same seven notes."

Richard Rogers, composer

✴

"Seven times tried that judgment is

That did never choose amiss.

Some there be that shadows kiss,

Such have but a shadow's bliss."

William Shakespeare, 1564-1616, in *The Merchant of Venice*

✴

"The seven deadly sins ... food, clothing, firing, rent, taxes, respectability, and children. Nothing can lift those seven millstones from

Man's neck but money; and the spirit cannot soar until the millstones are lifted."

George Bernard Shaw, 1856-1950, in *Major Barbara*

"The seven deadly sins: Want of money, bad health, bad temper, chastity, family ties, knowing that you know things, and believing in the Christian religion."

Samuel Butler, 1835-1902, in *Samuel Butler's Notebook*

"Once in seven years I burn all my sermons; for it is a shame if I cannot write better sermons now than I did seven years ago."

John Wesley, 1703-1791

"I have lost my seven best friends, which is to say God has had mercy on me seven times without realizing it. He lent a friendship, took it from me, sent me another."

Jean Cocteau

"In the 1940s a survey listed the top seven discipline problems in public schools: talking, chewing gum, making noise, running in the halls, getting out of turn in line, wearing improper clothes, not putting paper in wastebaskets. A 1980s survey lists these top seven: drug abuse, alcohol abuse, pregnancy, suicide, rape, robbery, assault."

George F. Will

✳

"He will deliver you from six troubles; in seven no harm shall touch you."

The Holy Bible, Job 5:19

✳

"These six things doth the Lord hate: yea, seven are an abomination unto him: A proud look, a lying tongue, and hands that shed innocent blood, a heart that deviseth wicked imaginations, feet that be swift in running into mischief, a false witness that speaketh lies, and he that soweth discord among brethren."

The Holy Bible, Proverbs 6:16

✳

"I can't write five words but that I change seven."

Dorothy Parker

✳

In *The Sign of Four*, Sherlock Holmes shoots up, and when questioned, replies: "It is cocaine... a seven-per-cent solution. Would you care to try it?"

Arthur Conan Doyle

✳

"I have heard the pigeons of the Seven Woods

Make their faint thunder, and the garden bees

Hum in the line-tree flowers; and put away

The unavailing outcries and the old bitterness

That empty the heart."

William Butler Yeats, 1865-1939, from "In the Seven Woods"

✳

"I must be like the princess who felt the pea through seven mattresses; each book is a pea."

C. S. Forester

✳

"Seven cities warred for Homer, being dead,

Who, living, had no roof to shroud his head."

Thomas Heywood, 1574-1641, in *Hierarchie of the Blessed Angells*

✳

"I am the owner of the sphere,

Of the seven stars and the solar year,

Of Caesar's hand, and Plato's brain,

Of Lord Christ's heart, and Shakespeare's strain."

Ralph Waldo Emerson, 1803-1882, in *History*

✳

"Out of all those centuries the Greeks can count seven sages at the most, and if anyone looks at them more closely I swear he'll not find so much as a half-wise man or even a third of a wise man among them."

Desiderius Erasmus, 1466-1536, in *Praise of Foll*

"Seven years would be insufficient to make some people acquainted with each other, and seven days are more than enough for others."

Jane Austen, 1775-1817, in *Sense and Sensibility*

"A people is a detour of nature to get six or seven great men. Yes, and then to get around them."

Freidrich Nietzsche, 1844-1900, in *Beyond Good and Evil*

"I am sometimes told that 'Women ain't fit to vote. Why, don't you know that a woman has seven devils in her: and do you suppose a woman is fit to rule the nation?' Seven devils ain't no account; a man has a legion in him."

Sojourner Truth, 1797-1883

"You can get awfully famous in this country in seven days."

Gary Hart

"He writes free verse, I'm told, and he is thought to be the author of the Seven Freedoms: free will, trade, verse, thought, love, speech, coinage."

Robert Frost, 1874-1963, in *How Hard It Is to Keep from Being Kings When It's in You and in the Situation*

"If I get a hard audience they are not going to get away until they laugh. Those seven laughs a minute—I've got to have them."

Ken Dodd

"The human mind is like Salome at the beginning of dance, hidden from the outside world by seven veils. Veils of reserve, shyness, fear."

Muriel Box, British screenwriter

"Let every man be master of his time till seven at night."

William Shakespeare, 1564-1616, in *Macbeth*

"Insanity is a contagious disease, so my healing belonged to everyone, and my victory was proof that the Negro has seven spleens and does not just give up like that, at the first sign of trouble."

Simone Schwarz-Bart, in *The Bridge of Beyond*

"How can man know himself? He is a dark and hidden thing; whereas the hare is said to have seven skins, man can take off seven times seventy skins and still not be able to say 'That is you as you really are.'"

Friedrich Nietzsche, 1844-1900

"Fives, and tens,

Threes and fours and twelves,

All the volte face of decimals,

The whirligig of dozens and the pinnacle of seven."

D. H. Lawrence, 1885-1930, in *Tortoise-Shell*

"Who clipped the lion's wings

And flea'd his rump and pared his claws?

Thought Burbank, meditating on

Time's ruins, and the seven laws."

T. S. Eliot, 1888-1965, in *Burbank with a Baedeker: Bleistein with a Cigar*

"The boys are in such a mood that if someone introduced the Ten Commandments, they'd cut them down to seven."

Norris Cotton, US Senator

"Good sense, which only is the gift of Heaven,

And though no science, fairly worth the seven."

Alexander Pope, 1688-1744, in *Moral Essays*

"Most things are born in the mothering darkness and most things die. Darkness is the womb of creation, my boy. But the sun with his seven horns of flame is the father of life."

Zora Neale Hurston, 1891-1960, in *Moses Man of the Mountain*

"An average English word is four letters and a half. By hard, honest labor I've dug all the large words out of my vocabulary and shaved it down till the average is three and a half ... I never write 'metropolis' for seven cents, because I can get the same money for 'city.' ... I never write 'valetudinarian' at all, for not even hunger and wretchedness can humble me to the point where I will do a word like that for seven cents."

Mark Twain, 1835-1910, in *Spelling and Pictures*

"A country is strong which consists of wealthy families, every member of whom is interested in defending a common treasure; it is weak when composed of scattered individuals, to whom it matters little whether they obey seven or one."

Honore' De Balzac, 1799-1850, in *Letters of Two Brides*

On the number seven: "To attempt to cite all the things included in this mystical number would require a library."

H. P. Blavatsky, in *Theosophist*

"Nature delights in the number seven."

Philo Judaeus

"The only man, woman, or child who ever wrote a simple declarative sentence with seven grammatical errors is dead."

e. e. cummings, On the death of Warren Harding

"I have to admit I'm still at square one. Not that I really object to square one. It's the only numbered square in the game. At least you know where you are. Nobody ever screws up and goes, 'Well, back to oval seven.'"
Jerry Seinfeld

"The nice guys are over there in seventh place." (Often misquoted as "Nice guys finish last."
Leo Durocher, about the New York Giants

"All human actions have one or more of these seven causes: chance, nature, compulsion, habit, reason, passion, desire."
Aristotle

ORDINALS

The Seventh . . .

Amendment to the US Constitution guarantees the right to trial by jury in common law suits

Busiest airport in the world	Frankfurt Airport, Frankfurt, Germany, 45,858,315 passengers per year
Country with most college students	Philippines: 2,017,972
Country with most universities	Indonesia: 1,236
Country with longest coastline	Norway: 13,624 miles
Deepest cave, world	System Hauula, Mexico: 4,839 feet
Deepest depression on earth	Death Valley, Nevada: 282 feet *below* sea level
Deepest lake in the world	Crater Lake, Oregon: 1,943 feet
Deepest sea in the world	Bering Sea: 15,659 feet
Driest inhabited place on earth	Asyut, Egypt: .2 inches of rain per year
Driest place on earth	Iquique, Chili: .2 inches of rain yearly; also has the seventh fewest days of rain: two per year
Fastest mammal	Brown hare: 45 m.p.h.
Heaviest element	gold: 19.29 density
Highest mountain in the world	Dhaulagiro, Nepal: 8,167 meters
Highest waterfall in the world	Tyssestrengane, Tysso River, Nor-

way: 2,120-foot drop

Highest population density in the world   Taiwan: 1,591 people per sq. mile

Largest body in our solar system   Venus: 7,520 miles in diameter

Largest city by area in the US   Phoenix: 473 sq. miles

Largest city by population in the US San Diego: 1,238,311 residents

Largest city, by population in the world   Lagos, Nigeria: 13,488,000 residents

Largest continent by population   Antarctica: 0 permanent residents

Largest continent by area   Australia: 7,687,000 sq. miles

Largest country by area   India: 1,147,949 sq. miles

Largest country by population   Bangladesh: 158,570,535 residents

Largest desert in the world, cold winter   Tuklamakan, China: 105,000 sq. miles

Largest desert in the world, subtropical   Great Sandy, Australia; 150,000 sq. miles

Largest island in the US   Baranof, Alaska: 1,636 sq. miles

Largest island in the world   Honshu, in the Sea of Japan: 88,925 sq. miles

Largest lake in the world   Great Bear Lake, Northwest Territories, Canada: 12,270 sq. miles

Largest metro area by population Shanghai, China: 14.3 million residents

Largest national forest in the US   Humboldt National Forest, Elko, Nevada

Largest national park in the US   Lake Clark, Alaska: 2,619,733 sq. acres (Alaska has seven of the top ten largest national parks.)

Largest sea in the world   Sea of Okhotsk, Russia: 1,392,100 sq. miles

Largest state by area in the US   Nevada: 109,806 sq. miles

Largest state by population in the US   Ohio: 11,373,541 residents

Largest university in the world   University of Buenos Aires: 183,397 enrolled students

Least densely populated US state — Idaho: 15.6 residents per sq. mile

Lightest element — phosphorus: 1.825 density

Longest bone in human body — seventh rib

Longest cantilever bridge — Howrah, Calcutta, India: 1,500 feet

Longest suspension bridge — Golden Gate, San Francisco: 4,200 feet

Longest cave in the world — Siebenhengstchohle, Switzerland: 87 known miles

Longest city name in the world — Villa Real de la Santa Fe de San Francisco de Assisi, a.k.a. Santa Fe, New Mexico. The name translates: Royal city of the holy faith of St. Francis of Assisi.

Longest river in the world — Ob-Irtysh, Russia: 3,362 miles

Longest wingspan of birds — Lammergeyer: 111 inches

Most common cause of accidental death in the US — Home fire

Most common cause of death at work in the US — Farm and industrial accidents

Most common cause of injury at work in the US — Carpal tunnel syndrome

Most common city name in the US — Mount Pleasant, located in 38 states

Most common spoken English word — you

Most common written English word — for

Most common insect family — Caddis flies, with 10,000 named species

Most common motive for murder in the US — jealousy

Most common phobia in the US — vomiting

Most common reason for arrest in the US — aggravated assault; 185 arrests per 100,000 citizens

Most common reason for imprisonment in the US

Homicide: 2.2% of prison population

Most common street name in the US   Main Street

Most common surname in the US   Miller, with .424 of all citizens having this name

Most commonly use letter in English   s

Most dangerous occupation in the US   construction worker: 28.3 fatalities per 100,000 workers

Most densely populated state   Delaware: 400.8 citizens per sq. mile

Most influential person of the 20th century

Adolf Hitler (Time/Life poll)

Most inland water in the world   Indonesia: 4.88% of total area; 35,908 sq. miles (the US has the same 4.88%, but ranks first, having 292,125 sq. miles of water)

Most spoken language in the US   Tagalog: 843,251 native speakers

Most spoken language in the world   Russian: 167 million native speakers

Most water volume in a lake   Lake Victoria in Kenya, Uganda, and Tanzania; 604 cubic miles of water

Most water-flow from a river   Madeira-Mamore-Grande, from Brazil to the South Atlantic: 28,513 cubic yards per second

Most practiced religion in the world atheism: 150,089 followers

Most published author   Robert Lewis Stevenson

Most visited national park in the US Grand Teton National Park, Wyoming: 2,793,336 visitors

National memorial established in the US

to Thomas Jefferson, in Washington D.C. on 6/26/1934

National monument established in the US

Tonto, Arizona, 12/19/1907

National park established in the US Wind Cave, South Dakota:

1/09/1903

Nearest galaxy to earth	(tie) Leo I and Leo II: 750,000 light years away
Nearest star to earth	Sirius: 8.65 light years away
Person to walk on the moon	David R. Scott on the Apollo 15; 19:08 hours of walking around time; July 26-August 7, 1971
Planet with longest year in our solar system	
	Earth: 365.4 days
Pope, Roman Catholic	Saint Sixtas I (circa 117-126)
President of the United States	Andrew Jackson (1829-37)
Prime number	19
Smallest state by area	New Hampshire: 8,969 sq. miles
Smallest state by population	Montana: 902,195 residents
State with highest crime rate	North Carolina: 5,175 crimes/year per 100,000 residents
State admitted to the Union	Maryland (April 28, 1788)
Tallest free-standing statue	Christ, Rio de Janeiro: 125 feet., by Paul Landowski 1931
Ten Commandments	"Thou shalt not steal" (Ex 20:15)
Wettest inhabited place on Earth	Sylhet, Bangladesh: 178" rainfall per year
Zodiac sign	Libra

GLOSSARY

Al-Fatiha	the first seven verses of the first chapter of the Qur'an
beglar-bey	the ruler (bey) over the seven banners (government districts) in Turkey
ch'l ch'iao tu	Chinese; Seven Piece Wisdom Board; a puzzle consisting of seven shapes formed from a square
clove	old English, a weight of seven pounds, especially of wool or cheese
cubit	seven palms (the measuring kind, not the date or coconut kind)
cult number	any number, as 7, that has a "cult" following of people who revere the number to such a degree that they establish websites listing sightings and lists of seven-things
Dodonids	from Greek mythology, the seven daughters of Atlas; also known as Hyads
gogatyr	a Russian knight
hebdomad	Latin; the number seven, as in days; also, a week
hebdomadal	Latin; weekly, as a meeting recurring every seven days
hebdomatary	Latin; occurring weekly
Heliadae	the seven sons of Helios, from Greek mythology
hept	see hepta – this is the same thing, but used before a vowel
hepta	a combining form meaning seven; in chemistry, having seen atoms of something

heptachord	a musical instrument like a lyre, having seven strings; the interval of a major 7th; a scale of seven tones
heptacontillion	$= 10^3 \, (10^{210}) + 3$
heptad	a group of seven things; in chemistry, an element with a valence of 7
heptagon	a plane with seven sides and seven angles
Hapta Heando	seven sacred rivers, Hindu (see also, Sapta Sindhava)
heptahedron	a solid figure with seven planes
heptamerous	having parts in sevens; having seven parts in each whorl, like a flower
heptameter	a line of verse with seven metrical feet
heptparaparschinoch	German, the word for sevenness
heptarchy	a government with seven rulers; the seven kingdoms of Anglo-Saxon Europe
heptastich	a poem with seven lines
Heptateuch	the first seven books of the Old Testament
heptavalent	in chemistry, having a valent of 7
heptecillion	$= 10^3 \, (10^{51}) + 3$
heptekillion	$= 10^3 \, (10^3) \, (10^{51}) + 3$
hepteris	Latin, a galley or other ship with seven banks of oars
Hesperides	in Greek mythology, the collective name for the seven nymphs who guarded the golden apple given to Hera
Hyads	the seven daughters of Atlas in Greek mythology; see also Dodonids
hetmerfoldes csizmak	Hungarian, seven-league boots
Jentilez	aka Sept Iles, French for "seven islands"
jubilee	7 X 7 years; a span of forty-nine years
kora	a West African harp with twenty-one strings, the strings being "dedicated" seven to the mother, seven to the father, and seven to the child
La Vigilia	Italian; a Christmas Eve feast featuring seven fishes
mashie niblick	old term for a golf club having the loft of a 7 iron
Meamei	Australian name for Pleiades
mitzvos	a commandment; law; good works
nana	Japanese seven

ngoni	a West African lute with seven strings
Niobids	the seven sons and seven daughters of Niobe and Amphion in Greek mythology
palm	= 1/7 of a cubit
perch	antiquated British unit of measure used in masonry; equal to .7 cubic meters
positura	a punctuation mark that looks like a 7; showing the end of text
Qi-qiao ban	Chinese; a tangram
Qixigyan	Seven Star Crags, a Chinese landmark
sabbatical	a rest taken after seven year's labor; a seven-year time-span
saith	Welch; seven
Sapta Arania	Hindu; seven deserts
Sapta Dvipa	Hindu; seven islands
Sapta Loka	Hindu; seven worlds
Saptalochana	White Tara, a female Buddha portrayed as the seven-eyed Tara. Her "extra" eyes are on her forehead, the palms of her hands and on her feet
Sapta Parvatta	Hindu; seven holy mountains
Sapta Pura	Hindu; seven holy cities
Sapta Ratnani	Hindu; the "Seven Jewels of wisdom"
Sapta Rishis	Hindu; seven sages
Sapta Samudra	Hindu; seven holy seas
Sapta Sindhave	Hindu; seven sacred rivers (see also Hapta Heando)
Sapta Vriksha	Hindu; seven sacred trees
Saptagram	Indian city in west Bengal; name means seven villages
Sat-bahini	Hindu; seven sisters or maidens; deities of water
Satta-ussada	Hindu; having seven prominences of things sticking out, especially on a body
Sebitts	seven warriors, a.k.a. Pleiades, from Babylonian mythology
Sedemte Prestola	seven Altars, a monastery in Bulgaria named for the seven villages it is surrounded by, or for the seven military commanders who built it

sedma	Czech word for seven; also the Czech card game "Seven"
semanario	Spanish, a bracelet of seven bangles loosely bound together at one point
sennight	Germanic, unused; a week, shortened from "seven night"; also written as sen'night or se'n'night
sept	Latin; combining form meaning seven or seventh; contraction for September, which was once the seventh month
sept	Scottish; surname
septagon	a solid figure with seven planes – inaccurately used instead of heptagon
septamyosis	malady causing one to see sevens everywhere having great significance, resulting from disease or drug use
septaparna	a seven-leaf plant
septuagintillion	$= 10^{420}$
septavalent	see heptavalent, it's the same thing
septem	Latin, cardinal number seven
September	the seventh month of the Roman calendar year
septemfid	split into seven parts
septemfluous	in seven streams
septemfida	specifically a plant having seven parts
septemfluus	Latin; having seven mouths
septemgeminus	Latin; seven-fold
septempartite	divided into seven parts
septemplex	Latin; sevenfold
Septemtriones	Latin; referring to the seven stars of Ursa Major or Ursa Minor
septemvir	each of a group of seven Roman men of the septemviri, a college of seven people
septenarius	containing seven; a verse containing seven feet
septenary	of the number seven or a group of seven; in seven portions; grouped in sevens; of base seven
septendecillion	$= 1054$ in US; $= 10102$ in the UK

septeni	Latin; seven at one time; seven each
septennial	a period of seven years or occurring every seventh year
septenquadragintillion	$= 10^{144}$
septenquinquagintillion	$= 10^{174}$
septentrigintillion	$= 10^{114}$
septentrional	the seven plowing oxen and also the group of stars near the north pole known as Ursa Major; also meaning "of the north"
septemvigintillion	$= 10^{84}$
septet	another group of seven
septet	in music, a composition for seven voices or seven instruments
septenarisation	see septialisation
septfoil	in architecture, an ornamentation of a plant having seven lobes
septi	Latin; see septem above; just another way of saying the same
septimalisation	the adaptation of the septimal system for religious and physical measurements
septic	something rotten, having nothing to do with seven unless there are seven rotting things
septies	Latin; seven times
septilateral	having seven sides
Sept Iles	French; Seven Islands
septillion	1,000,000,000,000,000,000,000,000, but only in the US – the UK says it is 1 + 42 zeroes
septillion	$= 10^{24}$
septimal	of the number seven, again
septimal	relating to or based on the number seven
septimanum	soldiers of the seventh legion
Septimontium	a Roman festival of the seven hills of Rome. It was celebrated in September. They sacrificed seven animals at seven times in seven different places within the walls of the city near the seven hills.

septimanus   of the seventh

septime   the seventh position in fencing

septimum   for the seventh time

septimus   seventh

septipedalian   a person, usually a basketball player, seven feet tall

septnonagintillion $= 10^{294}$

septoctogintillion $= 10^{264}$

septomania   term coined by Marty Cooling to describe the harmless psychosis for all things related to the number seven

septophobia   fear of decaying things (just checking to see if you are really reading all of this)

septseptuagintillion $= 10^{234}$

septsexagintillion $= 10^{204}$

septuagintillion $= 10^{213}$

septuennis   Latin; of seven years

septuple   of seven; multiplied by seven; to make seven times as much; in music, where a measure is divided into seventh

seven   ?

seven   Australian slang, 60s and 70s, a seven-ounce glass of beer

seven and six   UK slang, 40s, "was she worth it?"; in bingo, the number 76

seven bells   any one of four different hours in a day, when using marine time

seven dials   UK slang, 70s, hemorrhoids (rhyming slang – "piles")

Seven Dials raker   UK slang 1900-20s, a hooker living in the Seven Dials area of London, but working in other areas of town

seven digits   US slang, 70s, a telephone number

Seven Mathani   seven often repeated; see also Al-Fatiha

seven pennorth   Australian slang, a convict sentenced to a 7 year term

sevendible   UK slang, harsh, severe, especially of a beating (seven double, or seven times, thus seven times as bad)

sevener	Australian slang, a convict serving a seven-year sentence
Seveners	Islamic faction
sevennight	a week; any period of seven days and nights
sevens and elevens	Canadian slang, "everything's fine" (from craps – as 7 and 11 are the best first throws)
seventhly	yes, there is a word for just about everything – this means "in seventh place"
seventillion	$= 10^3 * 10^3 * 10^{210} + 3$, or $10^6 * 10^6 * 10^6 * 10^{45}$
shichi	Japanese, seven
Shichi-fuku-jin	the seven household gods of good fortune
Shichi-go-san	Japanese festival; at ages three and seven, girls are taken to Shinto shrines on November 15
Shichi-ya	Japanese, seventh night; when a baby is names on the seventh day after birth
seibenmeilenstiefel	German, seven-leagued boots
silverweed	seventh bread; Potentilla anserina
tangram	ancient Chinese seven-piece puzzle; ch'l ch'iao tu; also known as qi-qiao ban
tanabata	Chinese, seven evenings
Tawaaf	Islamic, a form of prayer, performed by walking seven times around the Ka'aba
Telesphoras	the seventh Roman bishop in succession from the Apostles
Theon hemerai	Greek, "days of the gods," in reference to the nanes of the days of the week
thousand-septendecillion	$= 10^{105}$
thousand-septenvigintillion	$= 10^{165}$
thousand-septillion	$= 10^{45}$
thousand-septuagintillion	$= 10^{423}$
Tresaith	"town of seven," Ceredigion county in Wales
Tsat Tsz Mui	Chinese, seven sisters
Utukki	seven evil demons, Babylonian mythology
visiers	sages; seers
wasa wombe	African musical instrument similar to maracas, with seven concentric disks

Yaxkin	seventh month of Haab, the Mayan civil calendar
Yeditepe	Turkish, seven hills
Yom shaba	Hebrew, the seventh day or Sabbath
Zazpiak Bat	Basque, "seven in one", refers to the seven Basque territories

LISTS – A QUICK REFERENCE

Ages of man, per Bill Cosby — preschooler, Pepsi generation, baby boomer, midlifer, empty nester, senior citizen, organ donor

aki no nanakusa — hagi, kikyou, ominaeshi, fujibkama, obana, nadeshiko, kuzo Al-Fatiha; the first chapter of Qur'an "In the name of Allah, the Benefiecent, the Merciful;" "Praise be to Allah, Lord of the Worlds;" "the Benefiecent, the Merciful;" "Master of the Day of Judgment;" "Thee alone we worship; Thee alone we ask for help;" "Show us the straight path;" "the path of those whom Thou hast favored; not the path of those who ear Thine anger nor of those who go astray."

Amesha Spentas — Asha Vahishta, Vohu Manah, Khshathra Vairva, Ameretat, Hauvarar, Spenta Armaiti, Penta Mainyu

Apkallu	Adapa, U-an duga, E-me-duga, En-me-bulaga, En-me-galama, An-En-lida, Utu-abzu
Archangels	Chameul, Gabriel, Jophiel, Michael, Raphael, Uriel, Aadkiel; OR: Michael, Gabriel, Lamael, Raphael, Zachariel, Anael, Oriphel
Arits, doorkeepers	Sekhet-her-asht-aru, Unhat, Unenhauatu-ent-penui, Khesef-her-asht-kheru, Ankhf-em-fent, Atek-tau-kehaq-kheru, Sekhmet-em-tse-sen
Arits, watchers	Smetti, Seqt-her, Seres-her. Seres-tepu, Shabu. An-her, Aa-maa-khemi
Arits, Harolds	Hakheru, Ust, Aa, Khesef-at, Teb-her-kha-kheft, Ates-her-she, Khesef-khemi
Aspects of the Manifestation, Sufism	stars, moon, sum, rain material, vegetable, animal, man
Beatitudes, Bible	Rev. 1:3, 14:13, 16:15, 19:9, 20:6, 22:7, 22:14
Canary Islands	Teneriffe, Palma, Gomera, Hierro, Grand Canary, Lanzarote, Fuerteventura
Cardinal Virtues	faith, hope, charity, prudence, justice, temperance, fortitude
Chakras, Hindu	Muladhara, Swadhistana, Manipure, Anahata, Vishuddha, Ajna, Sahasrara

Champions of Christendom	St. George of England, St. Andrew of Scotland, St. Patrick of Ireland, St. David of Wales, St. Denis of France, St. James of Spain, St. Anthony of Italy
Chicago Seven	Rennie Davis, Tom Hhayden, Abbie Hoffman, Jerry Rubin, David Dellinger, John Froines, Lee Weiner
Churches in Asia Minor	Ephesus, Smyra, Pergamum, Thyatira, Sardis, Philadelphia, Laodicea
Colleges, Ivy League	Brow, Columbia, Cornell, Harvard, Pennsylvania, Princeton, Yale
Colleges, Montana's Seven Tribal	Blackfeet Community College, Dull Knife Memorial College, Fort Belknap College, Fort Peck Community College, Little Big Horn College, Salish Kootenai College, Stone Child College
Colleges, Seven Sisters	Barnard, Bryn Mawr, Mont Holyoke, Radcliff, Smith, Vassar, Wellesley
Colors in the visible spectrum	red, orange, yellow, green, blue, indigo, violet
Continents	Africa, Antarctica, Asia, Australia, Europe, North America, South America
Cosmic plans, Sufism	Zat, Ahadiat, Vahdat, Vahdamiet, Arwah, Ajsam, inseam

Daevas

Aesma Daeva, Aka Manah, Indra, Nanghaithya, Saurva, Tawrich, Zarich

Deadly sins,
per George Bernard Shaw

food, clothing, firing, rent, taxes, respectability, children

Deadly sins, Roman Catholic

pride, envy, wrath, sloth, avarice, gluttony, lust

Dwarfs, from *Snow White...*

Bashful, Doc, Dopey, Grumpy, Happy, Sleepy, Sneezy (named by Disney not the Grimm Brothers)

Factors of enlightenment, Zen

mindfulness, effort, investigation, joy, concentration, tranquility, equanimity

Freakies

Hamhose, Gargle, Cowmumble, Grumble, Goody-Goody, Sorkeldorf, BossMoss

Friendship 7, American astronauts

John Glenn, Alan Shepard, Walter Schirra, Scott Carpenter, Gordon Cooper, Virgil Grissom, Donald Slayton

Fruits of Israel

barley, grapes, figs, pomegranates, olives, dates, wheat

Fruits, in Hawaiian Punch

apple, apricot, guava, orange, papaya, passion fruit, pineapple

Gods of Creation, Mayan

An (god of heaven), Ninmah (goddess of earth), Enlil (god of Air), Enki (god of the sea and wisdom), Nanna (god of the moon), Utu (god of the Sun and justice), Inanna

(goddess of love and war)

Great green glens of Leitrim — Glencar, Glenfarne, Genaniff, Glenboy, Glenkeel, Gleniff, Glenade

Hathors, Egyptian — Lady of the Universe, Sky-Storm, You from the Land of Silence, You from Khemmis, Red-Haif, Bright Red, Your Name Flourishes through Skill

Heliadae — Ochimus, Cercaphus, Macareus, Actis, Tenages, Tiopas, Candalus

Hells, Hindu — Putra, Avichi, Samhata, Tamisra, Rijisha, Kudmala, Kakola

Hells, Islam — Gehennan, Ladha, Hatorna, Sair, Sakar, Jahim, Hawiyat

Heptarchy, kingdoms of Anglo-Saxon — Northumbria, East Anglia, Mercia, Essex, Sussex, Wessex, Kent

Heptateuch — Genesis, Exodus, Leviticus, Numbers, Deuteronomy, Joshua, Judges

Hills, Cincinnati, OH — Mt. Adams, Mt. Airy, Mt. Echo, Mt. Healthy, Mt. Lookout, Mt. Storm, Mt. Washington

Hills, Lisbon, Spain — Castelo, Graca, Monte, Penha de Franca, S. Pedro de Alcantaia, Santa Catarina, Estrala

Hills, Rome, GA — Tower Hill, Old Shorter Hill, Lumpkin Hill, Blossom Hill, Jackson Hill, Mt. Aventine, Myrtle

Hills, Rome, Italy	Aventine, Caelian, Capetoline, Esquiline, Palaline, Quarinal, Vinimal
Initiatory Grades, Mithra	raven, griffon, soldier, lion, Persian, Heliodrome, father
Joys of Mary, Roman Catholic	the Annunciation, Visitation, birth of Jesus, Adoration of the Magi, finding the Child Jesus in the temple, the Resurrection of Jesus, the Assumption of Mary and her Coronation in heaven
Kings of Rome	Romulus, Numa Pompilius, Tullus Hostilius, Ancus Martins, Tarquinius Priscus, Servius Tillius, Tarquinius Superbus
Lamps of Architecture, John Ruskin	sacrifice, truth, power, beauty, life, memory, obedience
Liberal Arts, classical education	grammar, rhetoric, logic, arithmetic, geometry, music, harmonics, astronomy
Nanakusa	seri, nazuna, hahakogusa, akobe, hotokenoza, kabu, daikon
Noahchide laws, Jewish	forbidden are: idolatry, incest and adultery, murder, cursing in God's name, theft, eating meat; courts of law are to be established
P.E.O. founders	Alice Coffin, Alice Bird, Hettie Briggs, Suela Pearson, Franc Roads, Ella Stewart

Parameters of musical notation	pitch, duration, articulation, tempo, dynamics, silence, timber
Pleiades	Asterope, Celaeno, Electra, Halcyone, Maia, Merope, Taygete
Psalms of Penitence, Bible	6, 31, 37, 50, 101, 129, 142
Rabbinic Commandments	saying blessing before experiencing worldly pleasure, washing hands before a meal, lighting Sabbath and festival candles, saying the Hallel psalms of praise, lighting Chanukah candles, reading the Megillah on Purim, establishing Sabbath travel boundaries
Republic of Abkhazia	Dal-Ts'abal, Pshay-Aybga, Sadzen, Bzyp, Gomaa, Abzhwa, Samurzaq'an
Rituals of the Sioux	guards of the soul, rite of purification, entreaty of a vision, dance face to the sun, rites of puberty, political alliance, games of the ball
Road Shows, Hope and Cosby	to Zanzibar, to Singapore, to Rio, to Bali, to Utopia, to Morocco, to Hong Kong
Robbers, Seven	Saturninus, Insischolus, Faustianus, Januarius, Marsalius, Euhrasius, Mammius
Roman numerals, letters used as	I (1), V (5), X (10), L (50), C (100), D (500), M (1,000)

Rules of Hillel, Jewish

Kal V'Khomer, G'zerah Shavah, Binyan ab mikathub echad, Binyab ab mishene Kethubim, Kelal uferat, Kayotze bo mimekom akhar, Davar hilmad me'anino

Sacraments, Roman Catholic

baptism, confirmation, Eucharist, penitence, unction of the patients, order, marriage

Sacred books

Bible, Eddas, Five Kings, Koran, Tri Pitikes, Three Vedas, Zendavesta

Sages of the Bamboo Grove

Ruan Ji, Xi Kan, Shan Tao, Liu Ling, Ruan Xian, Xiang Xiu, Wang Rong

Sages of Greece

Bias of Priene, Chilon of Sparta, Cleobulus of Lindos, Periander of Corinth, Pittacos of Mitylene, Son of Athens, Thales of Miletos

Sapta Badri, Hindu holy shrines

Sri Badrinath Dham, Adi Badri, Briddha Badri, Bhaviswa Badri, Yog Badri, Adi Badri, Nrisingha Badri

Sapta Dvipa, Hindu sacred islands

Plaxa, Shalmal, Kusha, Krauncha, Shaka, Pushkara, Jambu

Saptaganga, Hindu rivers of life

Vagirathi, Briddhaganga, Kalindi, Saraswati, Kaveri, Narmada, Veni

Sapta Puri

Kashi, Kanchipuram, Mayapuri, Ayodhyapuri, Dwarkapuri, Mathurapuri, Avantikapuri

Sapta Punya Nadi, Hindu sacred rivers

Ganga, Yamuna, Godavari Saraswati, Narmada, Sindhu, Kaveri

Sapta Ratnani, Hindu jewels of wisdom	rebirth, the law of cause and effect, everything exists in everything else, the essential characteristic of all beings, evolution and involution, the way to immorality and self-preservation, knowing yourself
Sapta Rishis	Gautama, Bharadvaja, Vishvamitra, Jamadagni, Vashishtha, Kashyapa, Atri
Sapta Saraswati, Hindu rivers of knowlege	Suprabha, Kanchanakhi, Vishal, Manorama, Bhagawati, Suranu, Vindodhaka
Saptagram, Seven Villages of India	Bansberia, Kristapur, Basudepur, Nityanandapur, Sibpur, Sambachora, Baladghati
Seas	Arctic, Antarctic, North Pacific, South Pacific, North Atlantic, South Atlantic, Indian
Sebitti	Nergal, Ereshkigal, Gugana, Namtar, Hubishag, Ningishzida, Huwawa
Sedemte prestola, Bulgarian Altars	Osenovlag, Ogoya, Ogradishte, Bukovets, Leskovdol, Ahelen, Lakatnik
Senses, ancient	animation, feeling, speech, taste, sight, hearing, smelling
Sept Iles	Enez Bonno, Enez Plat, Enez ar Bruer, Melbann,. Riouzig (yes, Seven Islands has only five islands)

Septs of Leix	O'Moore, O'Kelly, O'Deevy, O'Doran, O'Lalor, O'Dowling, McEvoy
Septuplets, Humair family	Hind, Nail, Noura, Fahd, Salman, Sultan, Al-Anoud
Septuplets, McCaughey family	Kenneth, Alexis, Natalie, Kelsey, Brandon, Nathan, Joel
Septuplets, Qahtani family	Bandar, Haifa, Naif, Shaima, Avdullah, Abdulaziz, Sultan
Seven against Thebes	Adrasatus, Amphiaraus, Hippomedon, Capaneus, tydues, Parthenopaeus
Seven Lakes, Chile	Panguipulli, Calafquen, Rinihue, Pirihueico, Neltume, Pellaifa, Pullinque
Seven sisters, film studios	Columbia, Disney, Fox, MGM, Paramount, Universal, Warner Bros.
Seven-Star Crags, China	Langfeng, Yuping, Shishi, Tianzhu, Chanchu, Xianzhang, Apo
Shepherds, Jewish	Abraham, Isaac, Jacob, Moses, Aaron, Joseph, David
Shichifukujin	Benzaiten, Bishamon, Daikoku, Ebishu, Fukurokuju, Jurojin, Hotei
Sleepers of Ephesus	Maximillian, Jambichos, Martin, John, Dionysios, Exakostodianos, Antoninos

Social sins, per Mahatma Gandhi	politics without principle, wealth without work, commerce without morality, pleasure without conscience, education without character, science without humanity, worship without sacrifice
Spider leg joints	coxa, trochanter, femur, patella, tibia, metatarsus, tarsus
Stalin's skyscrapers	Moscow State University tower, Ukraine Hotel, Foreign Ministry headquarters, Hotel Leningradskaya, apartment blocks of Koletnechnaya Embankment, Kudrinskaya Square
Suicides, Bible	Abimelech (Judges 9:54), Samson (Judges 16:28-31), Saul (1 Samuel 31:1-6), Saul's armor bearer (1 Samuel 31:1-6), Ahithophel (2 Samuel 17:23), Aimri (1 Kings 16:18), Judas (Matthew 27:5)
Takara-Bune treasures	Inexhaustible Purse, Invisible-making Hat, Lucky Coat, Wealth Mallet, Ghost-Chasing Rat, Full Bag of Rice, Magic Key
Things Jesus said on the cross	"Father, forgive them for they know not what they do.", "Amen I say unto thee, today with Me shall thou be in Paradise.", "Behold my mother.", "My God, why has thou forsaken Me?", "I thirst.", "It is finished.", "Father, into thy hands I commit My spirit."

Virtues, Roman Catholic	faith, hope charity, prudence, justice, temperance, fortitude
Von Trapp children	Leisl (Charmain Carr), Friedrich (Nicholas Hammond, Brigitta (Angela Cartwright), Louisa (Heather Menzies), Kurt (Duane Chase), Marta (Debbie Turner), Gretl (Kym Karath)
Vowels, Greek	alpha, epsilon, eta, iota, omicron, upsilon, omega
Wonders of the world, ancient	Great Pyramid of Egypt, Hanging Gardens of Babylon, Statue of Aeus at Olympia, Temple of Artemis at Ephesus, Mausoleum at Habcarnassus, Colossus of Rhodes, Lighthouse at Alexandria
Wonders of the world, Man-made	Eiffel Tower, Empire State Building, Great Wall of China, Hagia Sophia, Leaning Tower of Pisa, Washington Monument
Wonders of the world, Middle Ages	Coliseum of Rome, Catacombs of Alexandria, Great Wall of China, Stonehenge, Leaning Tower of Pisa, Porcelain Tower of Nankin, Mosque of St. Sophia
Wonders of the world, natural	Grand Canyon, Great Barrier Reef, Harbor of Rio de Janeiro, Mount Everest, Northern Lights, Paricutin Volcano, Victoria Falls
Zazpiak Bat, Basque territories	Araba, Bizkaia, Gipuzkoa, Nafarroa, Nafarroa Beherrea, Lapurdi, Zuberoa

ENDNOTES

[1] "The Magical Number Seven, Plus or Minus Two: Some Limits on our Capacity for Processing Information," George A. Miller, *Psychological Review*, 63 1956, 81-96.

[2] Jos Verhulst and Peter Onghena, *British Medical Journal* (Dec 21/28, 1996.)

[3] Verhulst, J., and Onghena, P. (1997) 'Cranial suture in Homo sapiens: evidence for circaseptennian periodicity' *Annals of Human Biology* 24(2), 141-156

[4] Westby, K., *The Amazing 7-Day Cycle* (1990) Association for Christian Development, http://www.godward.org

[5] Donald R. Barber, (1997) "The Origin of the Seven Year Biological Cycle and the Expanding Universe", *NLO News*

[6] Wikipedia contributors, "Crystal System," Wikipedia, The Free Encyclopedia, *en.wikipedia.org/wiki/**Crystal_system*** *(accessed 04/09/2012)*

[7] Miguel Cavo Ramon, "Kleptarian Elements Tutorial", www.gr.ssr.upm.es/~**miguel**/rcii/general/**kepler**.htm *(accessed 04/09/2012)*

[8] *An Internet Encyclopedia*, OSI Seven-Layer Model (accessed 004/09/2012) http://www.freesoft.org/CIE/Topics/15.htm

[9] Wikipedia contributors, "Figurate Numbers," Wikipedia, The Free Encyclopedia, *en.wikipedia.org/wiki/**Figurate_number*** *(accessed 04/09/2012)*

[10] Bunker, Dusty, *Numerology, Astrology and Dreams*, West Chester, PA, Whitford Press, 1987.

[11] Wikipedia contributors, "Mersenne Prime," Wikipedia, The Free Encyclopedia, *en.wikipedia.org/wiki/**Mersenne_prime** (accessed 04/09/2012)*

[12] Wikipedia contributors, "Deficient number," Wikipedia, The Free Encyclopedia, *en.wikipedia.org/wiki/**Deficient_number** (accessed 04/09/2012)

[13] Numbers, What kinds of numbers are out there?,Khovanova, Tanya, (accessed 04/09/2012) www.tanyakhovanova.com/**Numbers/numbers**.html

[14] *Seven Towns*, www.seventowns.com *(accessed 07/02/2008)*

[15] Bill Cosby, *Time Flies*, Bantum, *1988.*

[16] Crosby Gaige, *Crosby Gaige's Cocktail guide and ladies' companion.* New York: Fireside Press, 1941.

[17] *Deep Down Productions,* What is Gamelan? Andrew Timar, *www.deepdownproductions.com/what-gamelan-a-3.html*

[18] Allaire, Gaston G. 1972. *The Theory of Hexachords, Solmization and the Modal System: A Practical Approach.* Musicological Studies and Documents 24. [N.p.]: American Institute of Musicology.

[19] Michael Gershman. *Getting it Right the Second Time.* Addison Wesley Longman,1990.

[20] *Segram's 7,* Information, accessed 05/31/2005, http://www.seagram7.com/flash/main.html.

[21] *id.*

[22] emailTeam@Nabisco.com, 12/24/2003.

[23] *Seven Cycles,* About Seven, History, accessed 12/22/2003. http://sevencycles.com/about.history.html.

[24] Meredith Vault, Senior Manager, Marketing, Seven; via email 01/21/04.

[25] *Remington,* Model Seven Custom MS, accessed 05/24/2004, http://www.remington.com/NR/exeres/00001513leqeaajkwrvvuhsf/RemArms+Rich+product.as.

[26] Henry Petroski, *The Pensil: A History of Design and Circumstance,* Knopf, 1992.

[27] via email, received 08/16/2004

[28] *Caps 2004 APN*, At the Auction, Mark Caruana, accessed 09/27/2004, http://www.capsnews.org/apn2004-1.htm

[29] *Credit Basics FAQs-Transunion.com,* accessed 04/13/2012, *www. transunion.com/personal-credit/customer.../credit-basics.page.*

[30] *Wall Street Journal,* Pick a Card Any Card, Alex Stone, 12/10/2011

[31] Marilyn vos Savant, *Ask Marilyn: Answers to America's Most Frequently Asked Questions*, St. Martin's Press, 1992

[32] John Ayto, *Brewer's Dictionary of Phrases and Fable*, Collins Reference, 2006 .

[33] Stanley Sturges, *In the Valley of 7 Cities*, Review and Herald, 1965

www.ingramcontent.com/pod-product-compliance
Lightning Source LLC
Chambersburg PA
CBHW060241290526
45789CB00001B/138